TRAILS of LIGHT

TRAILS of LIGHT

an anthology of poetry, prose, essays, & short stories

300 SOUTH MEDIA GROUP
NEW YORK

Hearts deserve to be found and filled. The Trails of Light collection shows just how meaningful the human bond truly is. The authors featured celebrate those ties by sharing their poems, essays, and short stories—whether that's through experiences they've had, are currently in, or unlocking a desire for their future.

On behalf of the writers, authors, and 300 South Media Group, I'd like to thank you for your interest in Trails of Light, for reading the stories shared on these pages, and for giving a voice to the words.

Jay Long

For more information on each contributing author, please refer to the ABOUT THE AUTHORS section at the end of the book.

TABLE OF CONTENTS

I'll sit with you in your darkness
let you feed from my light
together we'll find balance
with each and every bite.

—Michelle Schaper

SHARIL MILLER

MIDNIGHT MAGIC

The night started with a searing heat
Which sealed their unique bond making it complete

He saw her as a vision from afar
Branding her soul but not leaving a scar

Through the darkness of the night, it was the "true" her he could see
Though they had not even met, so how could it be?

The scorching truth of an undeniable attraction
Desire felt at that time was only a fraction

The soul can feel empty and in a lonely place
Longing for a companion for comfort and an embrace

How they found each other while adrift in the sea
Is like the mystery and intrigue created by Houdini

Kindred spirits each with a flirtatious charm
Revealing to each other their many layers while meaning no harm

She was called a rogue, a vixen, and even a mistress
He combined them all re-naming her Rovixtress

Their midnight magic behind smoke and mirrors
Will forever bind them well beyond time known as years

Sharil Miller

MY WARRIOR QUEENS

Aquamarine and Emerald… two jewels which adorn my crown
They are the most beautiful adornments enhancing my maternal
gown

There are not enough words to describe all the emotions I feel inside
Filled with never-ending love and overwhelming pride

So quickly these two beauties were all grown up, and I was wishing
they could stay
But they had to go out into the world finding their own way

With voices all around them telling them who they should be
They listened to their inner voices finding their own identity

With their intelligence, wit, grace, and poise
They navigate victoriously through the world's noise

They conquer life's battles by whatever means
I'm so very proud to call them my beautiful Warrior Queens

These two amazing women fight for what they believe in
Standing up for what is right with passion and conviction

In their lives, they've accomplished so very many things
But their best achievements by far are raising their three Warrior
Kings

Sharil Miller

THE MOTH TO MY FLAME

In the shadows of my world, I found myself lost
What were the remnants of my life seemed to have been tossed

My whole world was colored so blue
To my own self I had to be true

In the darkest hours of my darkest days
You appeared before me in a surreal haze

Suddenly, by someone, I seemed to have been found
On a path of risk, mystery, and intrigue I found myself bound

Inside of me at the very bottom of a deep hole
You ignited the smoldering embers of passion within my soul

The mutual attraction was too hard to deny
Even though our very best we did try

From the seductive dance of the burning fire
Rose the wisps of smoke known as temptation and desire

Temptation is often too hard to resist
Temptation is always there to insist

Escaped feelings were always a risk
So, tightly we gripped our hearts in our fists

But, the seeker of truth looks deeply into the eyes
Where the truth is always found and so are the lies

Each sensual rendezvous brought with it many things
But, none so dangerous as the potential burning of wings

4

In some mystifying way, we made each other whole
And, that is why you are the mate to my soul

In another time and another place
The moth and the flame can transform to be face to face

The addictive flame continues burning bright
Creating secret yearnings of return flight

But, in the end, is there really anyone to blame
For the reason you became the moth to my flame?

Sharil Miller

KELLI J GAVIN

ANYTHING

I would do anything for you
My love compels me
Encourages me
Drives me
Forces me
Binds me
Commits me
This love I have for you
A tethering
Yet a propeller
This love
Makes me do anything for you

Kelli J Gavin

ON TIME

Thank you for being you
For arriving in my life
Not a moment too soon
But right on time
For loving me well
For encouraging me always
For inspiring me each day
Thank you for paying attention
For being dependable
For always being right on time

Kelli J Gavin

ALL THAT I NEED

I have been led to believe after all these years
That you are a conductor of all that I need
Of what I crave and desire and search for
You are a furnace to keep me warm at night
The one that enfolds me in your arms
And covers me with your affection
The current that stems from you doesn't just attract
It summons me to seek you whenever possible
Knowing your presence is about to be near
Gazing across the room as you enter
Meeting your eyes and welcoming your approach
When my arms find you my body begs you to come nigh
Closer still I will pull you into an embrace
That fire that resides inside of you doesn't just keep me warm
It inspires and guides and provokes me to do more
To never stop giving and nurturing and striving
You incite me to always explore what's next
The driving force to take the next step
If I am not capable myself to do all of these things
I will continue to rely on you
I have been led to believe after all these years
That you are the conductor of all that I need

Kelli J Gavin

D.B. WRIGHT

BABY BREATHS

Lying here in fragile happiness,
Hypnotised by cherubic innocence,
I inhale the newness of your scent
As I press my lips to your forehead.

Your sleeping breath next to my nervous waking chest.
Your breathing free and light
as seraph sighs.
Full of future promise,
Empty of burden.
Just breaths -
- holding nothing more
or nothing less.

My own lungs bellow
Deliberate and slow;
Laboured and unsteady
Thick with creaking wisdom.
Tired and over-tested.

I look at you in awe
of the life which stands before,
And in ache
At the thought of pain finding you.

I do not want you to learn in harsh ways
As I had to.

Nor to only rise without any falls at all.
I desire to be your protector
With hope you need no protection.
My death holds no value to me
Next to your trembling fate.

I want the life ahead of you
To hold the same contentment
As these hypnotic breaths;
the dreamy ease of your breathing
To last forever.

The weight of the moment folds around me;
I am suddenly shrouded,
In realisation that you are the best thing in the whole world,
With no close second.
my own breath quickens
to meet yours
The beat of my heart flutters in fear;
I wonder between the beats
If either of us will be enough.
Who will carry who the most?
My energy catches fire on puerile flames.
I feel more alive than I've ever felt before.

D.B. Wright

GLIMPSE

I wish It was possible to rip out these eyes and play back their scenes to you. If you could see the world as I see it for just a moment; you, the mesmerising lead in an otherwise bland reality. You allow your imperfections to noose around your beautiful existence when you should wear them as badges of hard-fought honour. Apply them like war paint. Let them glimmer and shine with pride and without prejudice, for those sparkling flaws are you: the you that you are to me.

Give me your lumps and scars: let me kiss and caress them first. Let me read your journey in the bumps and blemishes of your skin. Let me hold your flinches and quivers and still your trembling trust. Allow me to bathe in that soul which others only ever see in glimpses and shadows.

Let me pat away your tears with my own cheeks so we share the pain as it falls from your oceanic eyes: our noses clash slightly as I press my face into yours: our hair flickers and dances together as it meets. Let our touching chests syncopate our mourning hearts, to beat together as lovers or warriors. Your tears are my tears: your pain my pain. Your rage and fury boils in my own heart and soul.

Allow the burdening load to fall away from your body as my bones bear your heavy woes. My heat will melt the shame from your pours into mine. Regrets and mistakes dissolve to nothing as our breaths rise and fall in tandem. Cling to me for as long as you need, grip my hands and wrap yourself in me, until you believe in yourself enough to own the world again.

11

Then, let me stand beside you in awe: revel in your grace and majesty. In the blink of an eye, ready to burn in fire or die by your side: or pull you back into my solace to heal one more time.

D.B. Wright

BABY STEPS

Sometimes, the weight of shadows press heavy
Shadows of the lost ones -
Angels you'll never know in the mortal realm,
Who I miss from the pit of my stomach,
And in my skin and bones.
Their memory dances on my goosebumps
And leaks onto pillowcases.

The mess I become
In these moments
Teeters on oblivion

I am loathed of myself;
Infected by demons.
Dreams are sluggish and dark,
Nightmares savage and cruel.
Life ebbs on around me like a current passing a drowning bird.
Breath is sucked from my trembling lungs,
Depleting my capacity to exist in little increments with each
exhalation.
Hope observes from long distance.
Happiness a fairytale held in other hearts.
The word 'self' divorces 'love' and 'care'
And seeks lusty dalliance with 'harm'.
Light falls away from me;
Only darkest thoughts remain.

But you;
There's you.
For you, it all subsides.
Already you have saved my life
Simply by existing.

How unwise I feel looking into your bright blue eyes.
Gargantuan caverns of unknowing resting upon my shoulders.
Inept and impotent, yet ready to try -
To keep trying.

We both cry, head touching head:
You, for the things you need to survive.
Me, for the things that didn't.

D.B. Wright

JOHN SWEIGERT

JUST TAKE MY HAND

Tell me, as you look in the mirror,
What you see looking back at you.
Throughout the years of your life,
Know what they have taught you.
Your true innocence needs not die,
For your dreams, never be lost.
I can assure you if you wish,
To never feel lost, ever again.
We recall the feeling of loneliness,
But we never need feel it again.
I will gladly stand by your side,
No matter the storm or problem.
You can run to me when you wish,
Whenever it is too much to bear.
I am waiting outside your door,
I am just waiting for you.
Hopefully, sooner than later,
You will open up and let me in.
Without hesitation or holding back,
You can let it go and enter true love.
You are on the track at this moment,
It's just a matter of time if you allow it.
So my dear, just hold on,
It could be closer than you think.

You are there my dear, on the brink,
Something beautiful is on the way.
Your tomorrow will be better than today,
Just take my hand and you will see.

John Sweigert

MY CANDLE FLAME

In the middle of the night,
Sheers flutter by the window.
They are moved about,
By a nightly cool breeze.
Candlesticks stand tall,
Flames flutter, casting shadows.
It seems the world is not the same,
But I know nothing has changed.
I know nothing is left behind,
It is just a simple state of mind.
Standing up just a bit taller,
Allows for me to be stronger.
Trying to break free from it all,
Something I must begin to try.
Is loneliness the reality of it all,
Will this pain slowly fade away?
It is so much more worthwhile,
For this time is so precious.

This night is longer than most,
Is there the strength to carry on?
As heat rises from a candle's flame,
I too feel as if I am floating away.
Staring out across the room,
I see her face in the dim light.
There she stands, an Angel,

I hear her calling my name.
In the glow of that candle flame,
I see you are the reason I stayed.
Flutter for me my candle flame,
Bring light unto me in this world.

John Sweigert

BRIAN BERRYMAN

TAKE ME

Take Me
Take me to the edge of tomorrow
Where this reality changes to dreams
Where your body beside mine
Dissolves into One
When heartbeats synchronize

Take me
Take me to the precipice of delight
Teetering precariously upon the edge
Teasing me with the thrill
As you join me in ecstasy's release
And it washes over us like a tidal wave

Take me
Take me to where your heart lives
Show me the things that matter to you
Where your soul takes comfort
What brings you joy and contentment
Because these things mean everything

Take me
Take me into your loving arms
Wrap me up in a blanket of you
Let me feel your love on a soul-deep level

Where we communicate with each other
Without so much as saying a word

Take me
Take me with you whenever you may go
For we are together in spirit always
At times apart physically but never truly
For I dwell in your heart as you in mine
A place filled with Love and Light
My Heart is your Home now

Take me
Take me Home

Brian Berryman

EVENTUALLY

Eventually
That's what they say
Eventually, you will meet
That someone
Whose scars match your own
Intensity matches your own
Heart matches your own
Whose soul matches your own
I stopped believing them
I had been around the Sun
Over fifty times
And that's when
The magic happened for me
I wish I had oracular vision
And could tell you when for you
But I can tell you this;
Never lose hope that your One
Is out there
They are looking for you too
Don't give up on them
Because they haven't given up on you

Brian Berryman

MAYBE I AM WORTH IT

I spend my days fixing things
But I never thought to fix myself
Years of being told
I wasn't worth being fixed
Made me believe the lie
Because when you get told
Or made to feel
A lie like that over and over
Eventually, you come to
Accept it as truth
And then You came along
And showed me what Love
Truly is and feels like
And made me believe I am worthy
Of being mended
You convinced me that the lie
Was just that

A lie

And together we started building
A foundation together unlike any
I have ever known
I still spend my days fixing things

But now I am one of those things
I am a work in progress
And maybe someday I will get there
With your help

Together, my Love, you and I

Brian Berryman

CHARLENE FOX

HOME

I finally found him, the other half of me. My soulmate, my twin flame. The one who called to my soul, and I heard you.

You too were looking for your second half, the missing part that makes you whole. Alone too long, you were ready to find your 'one'. You felt the tug on your heart, leading you in my direction. The universe had spoken, your wish had been granted.

Your soulmate, your twin flame. The one who called to your soul, and you heard me.

The tenderness in your eyes say the words your mouth is afraid to speak. you gently place your palm over the place where my heart rests, unbeating. With one kiss you breathe it back to life.

When I touch you, you feel the love in my fingertips, without a word having to be spoken. The tenderness in my hands matches the tenderness in my heart. You know my love is true and I will never hurt you.

Your hands are strong enough to move mountains and they move me in a way no other man could. With each touch from you, I feel your strength, and it makes me stronger. When you hold me in your arms, I know I belong there. I know that I am safe. I know that I am home.

Charlene Fox

OUR LOVE STORY

We met in the summer. It was an unexpected instant connection.
Some call them soulmates; others call them twin flames.
We were fine calling each other friend.

We both had loved and lost, we both had scars on our hearts.
But you wouldn't know that if you saw us together.
We were so carefree; laughter we hadn't known in years drifting all
around us.

By the fall our friendship had changed. We started to see each other
differently.
We stared at each other longer than usual. We would find any excuse
to be together.

Then one day it happened, underneath the oak tree by the river.
You looked at me, rubbing your thumb along my cheek.
'I have always loved you' you said as you brought your lips to mine.

Our fate was sealed that day.
Our hearts had finally found home.

Charlene Fox

ACCEPTANCE

And I stood there looking at you, really looking at you.
And it dawned on me I am seeing who you really are for the first
time.
I see the sparkle in your eyes, the glow on your face, a softness in
your features.
I vaguely remember seeing them before.

And you're staring back at me, really looking at me.
You see the smile spreading across my lips, my light getting brighter.
And I begin to radiate with a love I have never felt before.
I close my eyes and bask in the moment while I take it all in.

And as I looked back in the mirror, I finally found acceptance.
I've learned to love myself again.

Charlene Fox

TRACEY KOEHLER

PATH of the FIREFLIES

A hidden glimpse inside my soul reveals a new path, lined with fireflies to guide my way. The path is smooth and soft beneath my toes like fresh sand. I can feel it give way beneath my step as the flight of the fireflies outline each footstep in its soft glow. My mind is filled with childlike curiosity as I follow along, the sweet scent of blooming hyacinths riding the warm breeze beside me. I can hear the lulling sound of waves rolling into an undiscovered beach in the distance and the far-off cry of a seagull.

The fireflies blink in code, speaking a language only understood between them, as they continue to guide me along this path. I look behind and see my footprints following, fleeting glimpses of my past just out of my line of sight. The fireflies blink again in unison, and I look forward again, leaving my trail behind, along with any remnants of the past, dropping them along the trail. This path is meant to lead me forward, and I have no desire to look back.

As I walk further, I can feel peace wrap around me like a warm and comfortable blanket. Each step I take, I breathe in the calming peace and exhale my worry and self-doubt. I can feel bitterness and revenge fall behind. Regret and loss are replaced with eagerness and wonder as I continue my trek.

As the sun begins to peek above the horizon, I can feel the joy inside me escape into a smile, my eyes wide and my stride confident. The path begins to widen under my feet. My step turns into a skip and twirl along the way, the fireflies dancing to the song inside me. The sounds of the ocean grow louder, its rhythm adding to my song, the seagulls crying in its melody.

As the sun rises in the sky, golden and gleaming, I can see the ocean I have been hearing on my journey, its whitecaps crashing into the shore and returning out to sea. It is at this moment that I understand my journey, this new path within my soul. A journey of rebirth, of letting go, of coming to life, and I realize how blessed I am.

Tracey Koehler

GYPSY'S REVERIE

THE FIRST MOMENT

It was the first moment of the rest of my life...

I wasn't looking for you, though I see now that I had been searching for you all along--not quite sure that such a special creature could actually exist outside of my mind.

I had spent years fading away into nothingness, trapped inside a life that was perfect on paper but void of connection, love, passion, and everything that mattered to me.

I was just a shell of a person that day, the light had long since gone from my eyes; weak smiles a permanent mask to cover my barren soul, and a perpetual numbness that crept ever closer toward my heart's seemingly inevitable death.

I made my way through the crowd of people, my body drawn in by the music you were creating up on the stage. My heart caught the rhythm of your drum and I raised clapping hands skyward in salute of your complex melody.

And then it happened...the moment that divided my very existence. The life I had before separated from everything that would be. The first moment of the rest of my life...

I don't know if you saw the sun glint off the bracelets on my raised arms or heard the echo of your drumbeat in my hands, but you found me amidst the crowd of people, within seconds of my arrival.

Then your eyes met mine, though what passed between us was more akin to recognition of a familiar soul rather than the appraisal of an unknown stranger. Far more than a glance, once our gaze had locked it was as though a sequence had been engaged that would forever alter our lives' journeys; the universe shifted in that moment.

To this day I have never experienced anything as powerful as the smile you gave me in that moment. The force of it went through my body like a shockwave, finding the final unextinguished ember in the core of my being and I leapt back to life—alight like a firebrand.

It was like being struck by lightning: a complete shock in every way, life-changing, and impossible to ignore. I was no longer inches from my soul's death; it began to dance with joy due to finding its long-lost counterpart, insisting that you were already known somehow and that now found once more, could never again be separated.

My eyes sparkled and reflected the glow of the inferno ignited by the fire in your eyes and the warmth of your smile. Whether I willed it or not, my body and soul responded in kind. Smile for smile; fire for fire; truths acknowledged and exchanged between two sets of eyes that had never before encountered each other in this life, but appeared to be windows to the home of the other.

As my soul rejoiced—it being the first part of me to understand the significance of the moment—my body effervesced, electrified by your presence. The chills coursing through my entire being signified my physical self being in complete agreement with my soul's analysis of you being a man I wanted in my life always.

My heart, having suffered the most in the past decade of my life—neglect inducing an almost daily death—was also beginning to awaken, thawing from the flames steadily ablaze inside of me. Yes, even my battered and previously limp heart began to beat wildly in time with your drums; pounding and singing a brand new song, full of renewed hope.

Truly, it was all I could hear in that moment; the world around me had fallen away. I was entranced, you were all I could see. I marveled that the reverse also seemed to be true. I had been treated as though I were invisible for years; lack of attention and connection leading to my life force being drained from me. I had been unseen, unwanted, and unloved.

But there, with hundreds of people gazing at you in all your radiant glory, you had eyes only for me. You saw down to the depths of me, to the woman who had been all but lost, had been withering away in a gilded cage, and your eyes called to her. Bringing her back toward the light, drawing her away from oblivion and the darkness she had been dwelling in.

And I came to you. A moth to a flame that could not be ignored or avoided. My mind tried to caution against the chaos that would surely follow this moment, for we were each entangled in lives of our own that existed before this miracle that had just occurred. However, the desperate warnings of logistics and complications my brain insisted on giving were half-hearted, recognizing almost immediately the futility of protest.

Because I had been awakened by you, and could never return to the ignorant slumber and pantomime of life to which I had been subjecting myself for years. One look, one smile, and everything-- myself included--would never be the same.

It was the first moment of the rest of my life. Unsought, unexpected, and unimaginable. But we were magnets for one another, traveling across time and space to get to that moment where our soul song would be sung. Once it had started its harmony, nothing could stand between us. The details of how our togetherness could ever exist in this lifetime felt trivial beside the overwhelming realization that you were real and we had found each other. The one we had always needed but never known to look for, jaded and made complacent by the harsh reality of having traveled life's journey thus far without our soul's true partner.

And though we had not yet spoken or touched, it was inevitable; we belonged. The forces that drew us together were far more powerful than any obstacle that has come our way.

In the blink of an eye, my life was over. Something brand new was created; I was reborn as my true self and would never again be satisfied with less. I was certain my future would by necessity have you in it; my brain casually suggesting exchanging names as a good next step to forever.

And the music returned to my ears; the world resumed spinning on its axis, and time continued to tick onward. And there I was. And there you were. Finally.

It was the first moment of the rest of our lives.

Gypsy's Reverie

DESTINY KNEW

It was the love that never should have been and almost never was
But fortunately, Destiny knew better…
For these twin flames throughout the ages
Had been striving to be together.

The day was here and at long last, the stars had all aligned—
Two hearts in a crowd of thousands, finally able to find
The one person who they didn't know they'd been seeking all along.
Their paths had crossed, lightning struck, intensity so strong.

They locked eyes, and recognized, their lives would never be the
same.
Their hearts were in each other's eyes, love dancing like a flame.
Against all odds, they found their way into a journey shared
By the mirror of their soul, with every emotion bared.

Twin souls singing a song
Known only to one another…
Drawn inexorably, destined to be together,
On this side or the other.

Gypsy's Reverie

FREE BIRD

He was a free bird: a wandering, wild thing
Drawn to a sweet soul and the song she had to sing.
But he'd been lured into cages in years past,
imprisoned by loves untrue.
Never again, he swore, would he be trapped and so away he flew.
He feared that she was like the rest, and so he remained leery.
But she only ever wanted to make them a nest—
Somewhere safe, a place to rest,
When his wings grew weary.

Her sweet song told the tale of years held captive, too;
The price of freedom she knew well, but also its value.
She didn't want to hold him back from the places he might fly—
You can't contain a gypsy soul and she understood well why
He hesitated to accept that her love was real.
Trust and safety, without control, she offered to help him heal.
And because she never tried to capture him, he continued to return
To the nest she built for them, and he began to learn
That her patient heart had understood him perfectly.
He had no more need to wander, for with her he was free.

Gypsy's Reverie

MARGIE WATTS

DARKNESS to LIGHT

Silently I lay here in the darkness, listening to the sounds of the night. The gentle humming of machines, the quiet chatter of voices. As I look around, I can see the rhythm of my heartbeat and the slow drip of life going into my body. To the left of me is the beautiful skyline with the mountains off in the distance. Life continues to move at its own pace, it stops for no one. My thoughts try to go to a place I wish not to go. Counting each moment till death. Instead, I count each moment as a blessing. I remind myself of the people who love me and those that I love. The heartbreaks and tragedies I have overcome. Yes, life has not always been good to me but death is not ready to take me yet. So until then, I will live and live it well, until I have nothing left to give. Because even in the darkness, there is light if you choose to see it.

Margie Watts

JAMIE SANTOMASSO

WILTED ROSE
(*A tribute to Robert Frost's "Fire and Ice"*)

Some roses may wilt in summer's sun, and
Say the heat was a force too strong
The strongest buds and petals in the
World can only hold strength for so long
Will you turn cheek and let my red rose die; in the
End, life, and bloom return tenfold
In knowing my rose will live on past death, the
Fire of the sun will never have its hold
Some roses may wilt in winter's cold, and
Say that the blizzard was too long
In knowing that love can never be frozen
Ice will never take away its sweet song
From death is born life and my love is
What lives, I will always be devoted to you
I've felt your soft petals between my fingers, and
Tasted the sweet nectar of you too
Of roses that wilt I will never take for granted, my
Desire will lift a dying bud to bloom
I hold your rose close, next to my heart and
Hold my desire within until my tomb
With my last request, I'll water your stem
Those who deny your thirst be damned

Who leave you in the sun to burn, only do so in
Favor of earning judgement and remand
...*Fire* of the sun will never have its hold

Jamie Santomasso

DOWN FOR the RIDE

Ocean blue halos thrown out into the waves
They pull me to safety, save me from the sea
You're slowly towing me back to home
Nothing can touch us when you're with me

Lost in the past, like a book with no end
Elipses extending into the dark
Unable to forgive myself for transgressions past
Always seeming to miss the mark

You took my hand, pulled me up from the ground
Taught me how to forgive
Showed me my demons lived only in my mind
That I was worth more than their motives

Through your eyes, I found my purpose
I was never too far gone
My redemption was born when you saw through my pain
My only regret is I let it go on too long

Forward movement, leaving the past behind
Hand in hand with you by my side
Now that you've shown me the way home
Baby, I'm down for the ride

Jamie Santomasso

818

She sat, drink in hand
Waiting patiently for her suitor to show
It was warm that night; August twilight as the background.
As he walked toward her they locked eyes for the first time
Yet she couldn't shake the supposition that they had been here before,
together.
A scent of familiarity; honeydews and lilac,
It enveloped her and pulled her to the edge of the rabbit hole.
She was entranced.

In that moment they were the only two in the world,
Creating what would be memories neither of them knew they would
keep.
Engaged in conversation, locked in a hypnotic stare
Mesmerized by his gaze, she knew she was looking at the calling
card of his soul,
Eyes blue like the seas.
She ached to learn more,
To read him cover to cover
To memorize his prologue and epilogue
To recite his printed words.
For in those pages lay the keys, and he was eager to open the door.

Their pull was magnetic, an exigent force that could not be ignored
by any that came across them.
Intoxicating and lush
An intensity to behold.

He seemed almost tailor-made,
A gift,
As if engineered by a master sculptor.
Was this chance meeting more than serendipity?

Day turned to dusk
Enveloped in discord, they drank in the blueprint that elucidated the other.
As if learning a new dialect, but one all their own.
They were becoming one.
Without words, they adjourned.
The anticipation of the unknown awaited them,
Playfully taunting the pair as they departed with intent
Retiring to her refuge they plunged further down the rabbit hole.

Hours passed like minutes.
They indulged in each other as if they were starving for air,
alternating between profound colloquy and the language of lovers;
whispery gasps creating the soundtrack.
Drunk off euphoria,
Endorphins coursing through their veins,
High off their own supply.
He embraced her as if she had always been there.

A spark inside her ignited, "what ifs" were replaced with
unquestionable truths that neither could ignore.
Synchronicities danced in firelight.
His fingers traced her art-laced body instinctively, as if having done it
for years, burned into his memory
Their lips met effortlessly, reuniting for the first time.

She welcomed him into her with only a look
He swam in the oceans of her lust.
Drowning in passion they gasped for air,
Floating with the stars as one.

Her soul was unable to shake the feeling of home
A place she wasn't looking for, yet discovered regardless.
Her reverie resided in his arms
The personification of perfection
And she knew, this was beginning.

Night birthed morning
Refreshed despite not having taken in slumber
They were each other's rejuvenation.
The sun rays recharged their cores
The reality had not set
Their lives changed irrevocably
They were now on the path intended, mirrored, as if prepensed,
forever intending to lead to this moment.
The now.

Finally, they rose from the rapture they had woven hours before
Bedsheets strewn across the floor in fervor.
Locking fingers like ivy
Embracing as if it were their last,
Knowing it was their first.
Their eyes locked, sharing secrets they themselves didn't know yet.
Becoming, in its purest form.

As she closed the door behind him a wave of serenity engulfed her.
Peace.

41

Purpose.
He left behind his energy with her
A song crafted by the fates,
Pacing her vibration perfectly in time
And she realized this was indeed beginning.
It had always been.

Jamie Santomasso

NICOLE CARLYON

CATALYST

I was walking through life
Oblivious
Then I met you
My existence crumbled
Still to this day
I am rebuilding
Every molecule
each cell
Rebirth has never looked so inspiring
You
A catalyst
My awakening
Thank you

Nicole Carlyon

SELF LOVE

I refuse to give myself a label
Define me
for the world to see
I have learnt to love the skin
that houses my soul
I have learnt to appreciate the real me

Nicole Carlyon

LOVE of SELF

A feeling of complete acceptance
wraps itself around me
Through me
What miracles transpire
When you love yourself
infinitely

Nicole Carlyon

MICHELE McKENNA

SHOW HER

And if you show her anything...show her honesty when all she knew was half-truths. Show her raw deep love, when all she knew was love that never matched hers. Show her she doesn't always have to be strong, that she can break down. She doesn't have to hide or keep anything in like she's used to doing. Show her you'll never look down on her or view her as weak when she does break down with you. Show her that she can tell you anything without judgment. She was always afraid of that with everyone. That's why she is quiet at times. Show her she can be open with you about anything that's bothering her, even if you feel it's small because trust me...even small to her is big. Show her an effort that matches hers. Show her how much you think about her during your day, because God knows she needs to hear it. Even if she knows you do. Even the strong can be insecure and need reassuring. Show her you want her and desire her. More than anyone. Ever. Thinking about what you'll do to her next time you meet. Show her she's a priority because you know you are hugely a priority to her. Show her you'll always make time for her when she had to be the initiator to make plans with others as long as she can remember. Which made her feel bad, but she would never let that on to anyone. Show her your dark, because you know once you show her all these things and she trusts you like no other...you'll not only see her endearing light but the addicting dark inside her.

Michele McKenna

SAFE

When did she feel the safest? The most secure? When she was with him. Yes, she was always a strong-willed girl, taking no crap, being the strong one for everyone. That was the role she took on all her life happily. It was part of her makeup. She knew no other way to be. Yet, what was behind all that strong exterior? A fragile delicate soul that questioned everything, over-thought what someone said and how they said it. She was smart and confident, yet not full of herself. Confident, but had so many dancing insecurities within her. Insecurities that were unfounded, but needed reassuring every once in a while. Trauma does that to a person. There were times he initiated saying things to reassure her and make her smile. Sometimes out of the blue which just made her beam. Other times, she just outright asked him. Not because she didn't know the answer, but simply because she just wanted to hear it. Hearing him say how he felt about her and things within the confines of their relationship made her smile, feel loved, and secure. She can be feeling insecure and uneasy because of her own over-thinking one minute, and then totally reassured and at ease in the next- just from a few simple words from him. Sometimes he even felt it from afar while he was at work. He just felt something. He knew. She didn't even have to say a word. Other times, she asked for that little reassurance by asking 'Miss me? How much? Love me immensely? What will you do to me next time you see me?' Answers he happily gave her quickly and easily because they were all true. All deep within him. She knew that. She knew his feelings, emotions, wants, and desires. But to a woman, knowing and feeling it is one thing. Hearing the spoken words is another. Every now and then we need to hear it. Some girls, like her, need to hear things more often due to traumatic events and losses in life that broke her. Those things really take a toll on your thoughts and emotions, and you need more reassuring than the average girl. And that's okay. She thought it made her weak asking certain questions for reassurance from him. But she's learning it's not weak. It's strong because you know what you need emotionally and are asking for it. You know yourself and you're respecting your emotional needs. You're self-aware. That's strength through all the trauma. Asking for help, asking for reassurance from the one you love with everything you encompass- is raw honest communication. He doesn't view her as weak at all when she asks him. He views her as the strong woman he loves and adores, going through something emotionally hard, and will always pull her out of her dark spots when she asks or not. He's her safe place of no judgments, just love.

Michele McKenna

C. HAGE

BECAUSE I

Don't ask what if,
Stop overthinking everything that could go wrong
If life was all ups you wouldn't learn anything
What if leaves too much to think about
Just do it
Instead of the what-ifs
Instead of the pros and cons
Just do it
Stop asking what if
And instead, start saying because I
Because I jumped without thinking I fell
I fell hard but I learned something
Because I jumped I gained something
You don't gain asking what if
You gain doing
You gain failing
You gain succeeding

C. Hage

ANCHOR

You
My love
Are my anchor
Keeping me in place
Without you, I might just drift away into the open sea
But you
My love
As my anchor
You also have to power to drown me
With you, I might just pay the ultimate price
And oddly enough
I love you enough to accept all that this is and could be

C. Hage

ANN MARIE ELEAZER

SIGHS & SKIES

I knew one day those soft, secluded, fairytale-like places,
willowy honeysuckle and wildflower forests;
black sparrows and overcast days escaping to have tea on the clouds
would dance their way through a little girl's sigh
and a Neverland's sky to land on the pages of my soul.
Childhood is not always where we lay our head
or who tells us when to go to bed.
It's the magic worlds we create,
the imaginary friends with whom we stay up late
and the light we often find while standing
at the edge of storybook garden gates.

Ann Marie Eleazer

WHAT LIES IN BETWEEN

In a world often riddled with cries,
tearful lies,
and the rise of fallen love affairs,
he was a surprise bouquet of romance and wild roses,
sincere eyes and lips that softly landed me into poetic bliss.
Delicately climbing through the stained glass window of my soul,
he learned my colors and shaded in the missing parts in a way
I never thought I wanted, but deeply knew I needed.
The one who fell in love with my beauty,
my beast,
and all that lies in-between.

Ann Marie Eleazer

VICTORIA CORBETT

FOUNTAIN of LIES

There in the middle of fervent hopes
and promised kisses,
lies a fountain of broken dreams
and desolate wishes.

Filled with words of commitment, adoration, and trust,
Painfully they were insignificant,
revealed as unjust.

Meaningless words
were whispered with ease,
From the lips of blasphemy
content to deceive.

He eloquently said, "I will always love you, my dear."
Always versed in deception
and lies most sincere.

Now that he is diminished from her life,
she does not weep.
The emotional wounds,
no longer unfathomably deep.

Here lies a fountain of broken dreams
and desolate wishes
Her soul no longer caged, like a bird
by all that she reminisces.

52

Newfound happiness has come around
It's a brand new start
Perhaps it is her moment in time
to fully feel again with her mended heart.

Victoria Corbett

COMPASS of LOVE

Reality can be so much more difficult than what we dream or even at times, write about. But no matter what conspires against us along the way, neither of us ever wants to give up. I could not imagine ever wanting to let us go. You are my choice and forever in my heart, deeply embedded. You look to my welfare and continue to help me find my true path, even encouraging me to spread my wings to fly free.

You are the best kind of man, rare and so beautiful. I have waited so very long, lifetimes in fact, but I can't regret a second of it. For even at times when it has been excruciatingly hard, with the strength I have built has come real wisdom, and the ability to love in a truly selfless way.

I don't know what comes next, no one ever knows, but I am now at peace, knowing that I don't need to know. I only know who I am and why I love the way I do. Your heartbeat is my compass and will go to the ends of the earth for you.

Victoria Corbett

KATHY A. TATAY

MY AUNT'S GARDEN

I lie on the green grass under the velvety sky,
as stars drip into the fertile ground
The earth embraces me tenderly as a kiss,
as the night sounds soothe, and echo around
I feel the magic surge within unbound
as moonbeams and fireflies add their nightly sound.

I awaken slowly to the touch of morning sunshine,
shimmering from the tangerine sky.
The tinkle of glass chimes on the old wooden porch
gather reflections as they multiply.

Marveling at the familiar throb of earth,
and feeling the pulse of living things,
I wander into the front yard,
unbothered, I still wear my white cotton gown
and sit there a long while inhaling the fragrant ground.

My aunt's garden filled with flowers is shining with dew
morning glory, snapdragons, roses, and lacy feverfew.

Perfumed days I spend at the old farmhouse
forgetting, for now, the city of my birth.

Here I roam free as a gypsy child,
slumbering under the starry skies
waking in the morning to the scent of nature

55

And fresh-baked bread with honey butter
I laugh aloud sitting on the old front porch swing
as against my nose, I feel dragonfly wings.

Kathy A. Tatay

JENNIFER JENNINGS DAVES

I FLY FREE

Finally looking forward
Finally looking up
My head and my heart
Are finally on the same page
No longer listening to
The "I can'ts" and the
"You're not good enoughs"
I will take my place
To shine in the sun
I will dance in the rain
With laughter on my face
Taking chances
No longer terrified of
What may come along
Standing here tall
Determined to be strong
I will lift myself up
With wings of my own making
I will rise up
I will be my own champion
The shadows will no longer frighten me
They will not succeed
This race is mine to win
For I am the only runner there is

My life is for me to live
I need to more than just exist
Don't try to chain me down
This time
I refuse to give up my crown
So if you want to find me
I will be taking flight
For the race that is mine
Is mine alone
You can't live through me
I'm not here as a slave
I fly free

Jennifer Jennings Daves

THIS PATH of MINE

Slowly taking flight
Testing my wings
Stretching to see
How far I can reach
Gathering strength
As each new day dawns
Looking over the seas
All those trying
Just like me
Others taking flight
With their newfound wings
Soaring ever higher
Gives me momentum
To keep on trying
I cast out a net again
Bringing in a few rewards
Praise for words written
Penned from the heart
Rising higher
My wings getting stronger
Trying new things
Makes them extend longer
I find myself
In new surroundings
Those like me
Trying their best

59

Forging new lives
For themselves
Their words
From whom characters
And emotions grow
Staying aloft
Getting easier
As days go by
And words flow freely
Confidence weaves
Its way into my soul
Freeing me from shackles
Of self doubt and loathe
So as I continue
To reach for new heights
I look to the paths
Of those who came before me
Grasping firmly at
The trails of light
They left behind
The sparks that guide me
On this path of mine

Jennifer Jennings Daves

D. RODGERS

SACRED DUTY
          (Inspired by those who cannot cry… Yet...)

Please,
Let me take your hand
And allow me to walk down this path with you.
You are never a burden.
You never have been.
You never will be.
My heart aches for you.
I can't even begin to understand the how's
Or the why's of it all…
But I want you to know
It is my honor
My privilege
My duty
To help you carry your load.
And sometimes,
Carrying that load involves tears -
Tears that won't come,
For whatever reason.
I want you to know you are not alone in this
Because I have spoken with others
Who are going through the same struggle.
As I am writing this,
Tears are streaming down my face for you.

I pray you feel them
May you feel some release
And some relief.
The tears will keep coming
Until they start flowing freely
Down your face.
Never is this anything less
Than an honor and a privilege for me.
So rest assured, Darling,
This is my sacred duty.

D. Rodgers

OUR FRIENDSHIP

Looking back to the beginning of our friendship
I feel as if I may have made you into my safe place,
As I trusted you with my life.
You were the one I turned to
In moments of despair,
Uncertainty,
Insecurities…
You were always there for me.
I cannot, however,
Ignore the fact of when
I disclosed my deepest, darkest secret to you.
There is absolutely no doubt in my mind
That I wasn't supposed to do it.
I struggled to spit it out.
I hesitated for the longest time,
Fearful.
Fearful of the neighbors overhearing
Through our paper-thin walls.
Fearful of your reaction.
Finally, I made the decision to disclose
The information in my car
Away from anyone's prying ears.
I fought with you regarding the matter,
Scared to say anything,
Knowing I had to.

You decided to disclose yours first,
Something I had already gathered
From a previous conversation,
As an exchange for mine.
My,
How we made ourselves vulnerable to one another
Laying bear our hearts that night!
Possibly receiving rejection from the other,
We proceeded anyway.
I looked at you as more than just a friend,
As you looked at me as nothing more.
I can honestly say I never have had that type
Of intimacy with another man,
A friend.
God forbid what would anyone think
If they knew what you do.
You surprised me with your words of acceptance
Of me as a person.
You didn't change the subject,
Turn your back on me,
Or walk away.
You showed me love.
As someone who didn't share my same beliefs,
My same convictions,
You surprised me.
And yet,
You didn't
Because I knew I could tell you…

You were the one I could count on
When other unhealed moments
Reared their ugly heads.
I miss those times of running to you,
To be honest.
I had conjured some sort of romantic illusion
That was simply never there.
My traumas had caused me
To attach myself prematurely
And unhealthily.
I deeply desired you to be someone
You would never be
Simply because you weren't meant to be more than just a friend.
I was willing to throw everything out
In the name of love.
Something I had done from the beginning of almost every
relationship
For fear of never being accepted and loved
By someone who shared my same beliefs,
Convictions,
Hopes,
And dreams.
I won't go so far as to say I would do it all over again.
However,
Things may have turned out much differently
If I didn't do all that I did.
I don't regret any of it,
Really.

You provided me a safe place
To spread my wings
To try out my new freedom
Of being able to communicate in ways
I couldn't with any other male.
I learned self-compassion with you.
That is something I would never take away.
It has grown and will only continue to do so.
I still cannot thank you enough
For all you have done for me and my family.
I don't know if we will always remain friends.
However,
You did teach me how to fly, again.
And that, my Friend
Was what I needed…

D. Rodgers

STEPHANIE MUELLER

I AM YOU

I am You.
I was born a baby too.
Unable to care for myself,
from my family, I needed help.
Mother did all she could to give me life,
to protect me from the hell of war-torn strife.
But, when born in a land
where freedom cannot stand,
we prayed for Heaven to intervene,
for one day to escape the grips of death and poverty.

I am You.
My only wish is for peace too.
We were summoned here, to this place,
saved from harm by Heaven's divine grace.
Many years may have already gone
since this land provided your family a new dawn.
Yet, I pray that one day soon will you see
that when your family was in greatest need,
your neighbors met you with kindness and empathy.

I am You.
We have traditional clothing too.
A hijab or huipil do we wear,
however, no evil magic do they bear.

Reviving memories of a life we once had,
these fabrics wrap us in the comfort of our lost homeland.

I am You.
Our words have meaning too,
whether Spanish, Swahili, Hmong, or Pashto.
We share, we cry, we laugh igual que tú.
We speak of life, of family, of home,
of dear friends, and blessed times long ago.
Yet we hear you whisper, we see your sneers,
and the sting of your judgment flows our tears.
For we wish you understood, we wish you knew
your misguided fears cut deep new wounds.

I am You.
Our hearts beat in rhythm too.
whether Muslim, Christian, Hindu, or Jew,
the Spirit Almighty governs our world view.
Although the Higher Power's name may change,
the faith we have, the prayers we say,
to the Universe, love speaks the same.

I am You.
We will lead our families too.
We will always do all that we can
to shelter our loved ones wherever we stand.
We promise to open their minds
to the beautiful differences of all mankind,
to respect the unique in one another,
to honor each other as sister and brother.

I am You.
Every day we live our story too.
The chapters may vary in the books we hold,
but our tales still speak of triumph and woe.
I invite you to talk, to listen, to laugh,
to build a bridge with me, to forge a new path.

For, I am You,
And I am human too.
Please do not be fooled by the color of my skin,
the language I speak, or the places I've been.
We are all sisters and brothers
born of the same sacred Earth Mother.
So, please do not be afraid.
There is no need to fear or to hate.
For at end of the day,
you and I have a vital role to play.
We can learn from our differences;
we can dissolve the ignorance that is.
Hand-in-hand, we can break down walls.
We can withstand the storm;
we can rise from the fall.

Two by two,
we will change the world view.
For you are me…
And I am You.

Stephanie Mueller

BEARER of LIGHT

As shadows cast fear upon the night,
my Angels surround me in heavenly light.
Guiding me through the forests of darkened doom,
to a path where only the moonflowers bloom.

Timid was once the flame of love
when thoughts of worthlessness swirled heavy above.
Yet the song of love echoed within
begging to be set free, for the ripple to begin.

With each new encounter
the rhythm of my heart beat louder,
as beings in desperate need of hope
left their mark upon my Soul.

For then did I know…
I was the primrose growing through the snow.
I was the Earth Angel sent to heal the hurt below.
I, the gardener, was holding sacred seeds of love to sow.

I am called to be a Bearer of Light…
to welcome the lost, the cruel, the unkind,
to unravel the painful story held in their eyes
to be a voice in the silence for those left behind.

I am called to be a Bearer of Light…
to soothe the wounds that weep and cry,
to soften the cheeks the tearful rivers dry,
to hush the fears that wake our peaceful night.

I am called to be a Bearer of Light…
to know your sorrow, to stand by your side,
to feel your humanness, to understand your why
to teach you forgiveness, to watch you fly.

Even in doubt, I hope you accept
my hand offered to you outstretched.
For never will you walk this path alone,
together we will travel the journey home.

My heart will our compass be,
redirecting our Souls to finally see
buried beneath mountains of needless anxiety
exists the beautiful we were always meant to be.

Step with me now into the darkness;
together the monsters can no longer harm us.
When locked hand-in-hand,
fear no longer has the power to stand.
For even if we stumble, even if we fall,
we will rise again to answer Love's urgent call.

You and I will lay our insecurities aside
to let our Light eternally shine.
We will embrace our holy gift divine,
for we are called to be the Bearers of Light.

Stephanie Mueller

HEAVEN AWAITS

Tonight your eyes sink heavy into dreams
of ruffles pink and lavender cream,
frosting the sweet evening breeze
with kisses of your cotton-candy tease.

The ripples you send
extend a hand
inviting us to understand
beauty awaits beyond this land.

For tonight each shoreline hush becomes clear
a secret message sent for us to hear…
"Wipe your eyes and dry your tears,
For Heaven awaits beyond this Earthly mirror."

Then, with a fiery flash,
we glimpse the brilliant splash
and into darkness, you again disappear
leaving us to wonder here…
"Did Heaven really just appear?"

Stephanie Mueller

SHAWNA OLIBAMOYO

IMAGINE

imagine you
image me
intertwined
in the stars
of enchanted skies
as the universe
takes its turn
to define destiny
we blend
into each other
the swirl
of souls
of hearts
of minds
to become one
in the same
the simple kiss
that begins
the ultimate infusion
of you
of me
just imagine

Shawna Olibamoyo

LOVE FOUND US

Into the day
Into the night
Love has found us
With the guided light

It is what we have become
Together
Now as one

Our destiny
Of simple tranquility
Designed by fate
To open the magical gate

Dreams that have come alive
As our spirits begin to thrive
We follow the path
To wherever it leads

Planting and nourishing
Our forever seeds

Yes love has found us
That we can not deny
The flight of our hearts
That soar high above the sky

Shawna Olibamoyo

THE SEARCH

Will I ever find you
Will you ever find me
A lost soul
Floating across the sea
Through the storm
Through the rain
The sail stays casted
The search is not in vain
The waters may be deep
And frigid cold
But my heart will not pause
To find the treasure gold
The fog is heavy
Thicker than before
Unable to stop
Unable to shore
Whether it be day
Whether it be night
I will keep moving on
With or without light
I feel your spirit
Inside of me
Follow the wind
To wherever you may be
The search will continue
It will not end

Until I find you
My love
My best friend

Shawna Olibamoyo

APRIL Y. SPELLMEYER

CLEAR, SIMPLE, AND PLAIN

It seems like a lifetime ago
The time we spent together
Endless conversations
Laughter and memories made
We mended each other's hearts
Playing pool and drinking beers
Singing off-key and air guitar
Another quarter for the jukebox
Glycerine and *Anybody Listening*
Those were our songs
Our eyes would lock
Our fingers entwined
The world stopped
It was only the two of us
We sang that one lyric
The one sung a million times
The one which was our secret
way to say I love you
"Clear, simple and plain"

April Y. Spellmeyer

SUPERNATURAL ROAD TRAVELED

"Dad's on a hunting trip and he hasn't been home in a few days."
  - Dean, Supernatural

That line is what hooked Christopher and I back on September 13, 2005. What a journey we were about to embark on. I'm not just talking about just the show Supernatural but our journey which would end with Christopher traveling the stars and for me to be here these last ten years.

For almost six years Christopher and I would watch it together. It was our show. It was a show that meant family and where family didn't end with blood. After Christopher passed, I continued to watch Supernatural. For me, it was another way to be connected with him.

Tonight I gathered my strength as I took a deep breath and pressed play to watch the last three episodes I had been avoiding for so long. I know why I avoided it. Why I only watched the reruns. This was a chapter in the book of Christopher and me. A chapter I didn't want to end. I figured if I didn't watch it our chapter would have the beginning but no end.

As I cried through the last three episodes, I realized this was just another stage of grief I never experienced. An experience I will insert into the layers of grief I already carry. I'm not going to lie, it hurts, it hurts like hell. Grief isn't glamorous or forgiving and is forever surprising in ways to wound. A fresh wound is on my heart. I know I will need to find peace and peace will be found with time.

I don't regret this experience. I thank my Christopher for all his love and the memories we made. This was an experience where two soulmates found their little piece of heaven in a television series.

Until we're together again I will carry on.

April Y. Spellmeyer

SONG CHILD

Tonight as my youngest child and I were driving to get him earbuds. He turned to me and said let's play our songs and sing. Of course, I sing every chance I get even though I sound like a cat being strangled. But with him, he doesn't care one bit of how I sound.

He put his little hand in mine. We belted out the lyrics with the radio turned all the way up, windows down and the cool breeze running through our hair. For this moment, the world drifted away; people, traffic, stress, worries – everything just faded. It was just him and I.

We were still singing when we pulled into the store parking lot. As we passed people some of them looked at us like we were crazy, some smiled, and some laughed. But it didn't matter to us. This was our time together. Precious one-on-one time is rare since usually, it's all of us in the car.

After our shopping adventure he asked between songs why do I have favorite ones that I play over and over again. I told him each song has a special meaning, something happened to me at one point or another in life where a song became a part of me.

I told him some songs just speak to me. Where I feel it flow through me and sets my soul on fire. He said he gets it and gets me because we are one of the same. He said he feels every single word, every note deep in his heart.

He then asked me to play a particular song he loves. He sang it with every bit of his heart and soul. I had to choke back my tears because of the haunting lyrics which went hand in hand already in his young life. His hand in mine, squeezing it occasionally as if to say we will be just fine. I squeezed his hand back letting him know yes, we will be just fine.

April Y. Spellmeyer

IMPASSIONED HEART

EMOTIONAL GREED

Limits belong to the sky
Infinity to a deep soul
Clear waters chasmic
Dive right in and lose control

Immerse your thoughts
In words from my heart
My eyes speak the truths
Not betrayed by my lips that part

Hide no more
As forever awaits
It's ours to explore
Acceptance is all it takes

We are more than shallow love
That only meets the eye
We are the emotions
Setting a euphoric high

We are the empathy
Feeling without touch
We are the respect
That knows not to judge

We are the trust
That calms our fears

We are the destiny
Chosen by the universe

We are the stars
Dancing in the moonlight
We are the darkness
Giving birth to the light

We are the flames
Perfecting the fire
We are profound
Exquisite desire

Without fear
Without rejection
Without doubt
A divine connection

I need you to want
I need you to need
I need you to love
With intense emotional greed

Impassioned Heart

UNCONDITIONAL

Love him with your eyes asleep
With your heart, feel his soul speak
His language of a heart old fashioned
Of love and honor unconditioned

Keep his heart safe, your own within
Never forgetting, that even him
In the face of love, has to be brave
To fear and pain, he too was once a slave

Be his strength in moments so weak
Acceptance and love is all he seeks
Stand by his side, his hand in yours
When darkness in his cup it pours

Shower him with love and truth
For he deserves to know his worth
On days of his self-love's near-death
Love him more with each breath

Beautiful in his vulnerability
Give his soul love and stability
Show him trust in all the ways
You have been broken many days

When he asks for nothing more
Shed your fears unto the floor
Sit with him and bare your soul
For he needs you to feel whole

84

Your Hero, he should always be
This is what he is to me
Unconditionally

Impassioned Heart

RISE

That first time I saw you
I could not find my breath
I tried so hard to escape
Yet your eyes held me there
I fell for you

Between your heart and mine
That first kiss from your lips
Like we were trapped in time
Our souls in a total eclipse
I fell for you

Your voice, so gentle
Wiped away all my tears
The fear, all-consuming
After a thousand years
I fell for you

Waiting and hoping to find you
And there you were
A man of exquisite beauty
A soul bruised and broken
I fell for you

I fell, between your pieces
Your pain I could feel
A silent promise in my heart

Your scars I would heal
I fell for you

I cannot remember me
Without thinking of you
I cannot imagine life
Before I loved you
I fell for you

Separated by fear
Each day, such torment
Yet I cannot give up
My love for you, fervent
Still, I fall, yet I rise for you

Impassioned Heart

MEL

UNPANNED GOLD

The pain that rocked my existence
Still echos through the night
No interest in the days of shallow
Relying on my 3rd eye sight
Reading Rumi, Pema, and Tolle
Searching for answers in the dizzying prose
I search to heal what is broken
Without fear I let my cracks show
For its in humility, we find true freedom
With empathy, the heart of our own soul
With compassion, we halt the judgments
And with love, we fill all the holes
And sometimes when we pause
As we are still, quiet and stand on hold
We find the path to riches
Paved with unpanned gold.

MEL

THE TREE PORTAL

Come sit with me by the tree near the pond
And let's cherish the spell of this soul-felt bond
We can talk of life and love and all the things we feel
Of past lives together that must have been real
For this connection so strong, we need to explore
So in our next life, We find the same door

MEL

KALEIDOSCOPE

Leave a lantern by the entrance
For all lost souls to find
Let it shine into their sorrows
And release the ties that bind
A kaleidoscope of colors
To guide their way each day
To remind me of their courage
That got lost along the way
We all have felt despair and
Been faced with pain and struggles
But on the other side of darkness
The Angels remove the troubles.

MEL

LYSSA DAMON

I WISH

I wish
for your heart
a soft landing place,
for your soul
someone that understands
every nuance
of your being,
and a love
that hears the magic
in your heartbeat.

Lyssa Damon

ME

I will not
apologise
for who I am,
how I love or
hide the things
that set my
soul alight.

I will bask
in the flames,
my naked soul
on full display.
Shamelessly.
Recklessly.
Me.

Lyssa Damon

JUST LIKE THAT

And just like that,
she threw off
the weight of
'things the world expects',
cast her eyes
to the sky,
a smile dancing
on her lips
as she listened
to the tune of
her own heartbeat.

Lyssa Damon

SARAH HALL

CITY LIGHTS

I remember that night, you took me to the lookout of the city lights.
I remember your hand in mine,
as we sat in a comfortable silence.
Parked in the dark,
absorbing the breathtaking view laid out right before us.
I remember a certain feeling.
Like we were the only two people left in the world.
Survivors.
Who had somehow made it to the edge of the Earth.
That night.
The traumas we had lived through. Just didn't seem to matter.
The wounds temporarily closed over,
and the scars on our hearts invisible.
I've never been back there again.
I just cannot bring myself to do it.
For some memories are just too sacred to be tainted.
But I will always remember that night.
When it was just you and I, sitting in the dark,
your hand entwined with mine.
And whenever I catch myself wondering how I will ever muster the
strength to survive?
I always remember the lights.

Sarah Hall

STITCHES and SCAR TISSUES

Sweetheart,
you need to tend to those welts.
Branded and swollen
across your heart.

Bandage those blisters
on your cracked lips,
from loving them too much
and too hard.

Cripple those demons
by mending your sad mind.

You are more
than a wounded human.
You are more than
a pile of damage bleeding.

You are more than
the aches and the pain.

You will heal
and you will mend.
You will one day
feel beautiful again.

Carry those scars like trophies my darling,
wear them like war armour
and Purple Hearts.

With nothing but honour and pride.

Show the world courageously
exactly how you damn well survived.

Sweetheart, you are the stitches
and you are the scar tissue.

The nurse all night at your bedside.
The paramedic who brings you back to the light.
Be the Doctor of your life.

Sarah Hall

HONOUR HER

Honour that girl
who once upon a time,
jumped in puddles
and loved to climb trees.

Honour that girl
who craved adventures
and midnight walks
along the beach.

Honour that girl
who giggled with joy,
made daisy chains
and ran barefoot in the streets.

Honour that girl
who made mud pies,
and chased butterflies
riding her bike
in the cool summer night's breeze.

Honour that girl
with the crazy hair,
the curious mind,
the gypsy soul
and the sparkling eyes.

Honour that girl
who laughed till she cried,

who's future was bright,
who would dance through the night
and was never afraid
to stand for what's right.

Honour that girl
who you once were,
before the world told you
who you should be.

Honour that girl
who you have kept locked away,
for she is begging
to be set free.

Sarah Hall

VALERIE LEYDEN-MORFFI

CHAPTER 7: SAINT MATTHEW

PART ONE

From the first time I noticed him, something about him caught my
attention.
His voice captivated me, and his emotive words struck chords deep
within.
Interactions were kept at bay, however, while apparently false
perceptions presented as reality.
But that first time we messaged all night, oh how I felt the twinge of
disappointment having to say goodbye.
The next time was too much to bear, so I ripped the Band-Aid off,
inquiring about the wall I perceived stood in our way.
Inexplicable relief.
With the air cleared and truth divulged, a flood of hot emotions
washed over me as I finally allowed myself to succumb...
That night we blasted through the ice with an explosion of atomic
proportions.

In the wake of the aftermath, once the dust settled, it was quite clear -
we melded well together into something beautiful.
Like Hydrogen and Oxygen, we became one fluid body of water -
A vast ocean with profound depths and sweeping tides of emotion.

Both nothing and everything made sense.
But it felt like the Gods had answered my prayers -
He was everything I ever wished for.

PART TWO

Hours upon hours pass as mere minutes.
His voice still captivated me, but it's the sound of his echoing
laughter that lights me up;
The sight of his deliciously wicked and reassuring smile, framed by
two perfect dimples, that warms my heart;
And the way he speaks to me, with such conviction of love and
support, that completely melts me.

I could easily lose myself forever in that enamored gaze he holds on
me.

As each day passes, the yearning to feel myself in his arms grows
stronger, along with the swelling of my heart.
All logic and laws of time cease to exist for deep-feeling old souls.
The day we get to tangibly feel each other's warm embrace will be
here before we know it and feel like no time has passed.
I thank Odin every day for bringing me this incredible man - I know
exactly what I have.

And every day I look at this beautiful man's handsome face, stare
into his loving, brilliant eyes, and I feel it.
Every fiber of my being resonates with the knowledge -
It was always supposed to be Him.

Valerie Leyden-Morffi
(Whiskey + Empathy)

REBIRTH

Windows down, moon roof open.
The delicious night breeze fills the car, and I can taste Spring.
That earthy smell of recently thawed ground where daffodils and
crocuses have emerged,
white magnolias unfurled, and trees bursting with buds...
reminders of life, as rebirth takes center stage, her shining moment.

I catch a glimpse of myself in the rear-view mirror.
Strands of silver now infiltrate my raven mane.
Where has the time gone?
I hardly recognize myself sometimes.
So much has changed these past few years...
Immense grief, friendships lost, profound love found, relationships
gained;
a world pandemic and forced isolation.
There are times I find it hard to catch my breath, my dizzy head
struggling to keep up.
Yet for the most part, it feels as if this has always been.
Confined, in body and mind, I find myself shrinking away from all
that used to feed my soul.
Instead, feeding a void I cannot name, I grow,
taking up more space in this car than I used to.
My once flexible limbs grow more rigid by the day, my body betrays
me...
Or is it I who has betrayed my body?

Headlights blur past as I stare out the windshield.
The waning Moon, nothing more than a sliver, follows along,
mocking me with her crooked smile, like the Cheshire Cat.
Another trip around the sun I've made.
Another year of life I've lived.
Another number to my years, one so many are not as fortunate to see.

I am beyond blessed... motherhood, love, family, friends, work,
shelter, life.
Stuck in my head as I may be, I know this, and I know what I am
capable of,
what I've already achieved.
This is MY shining moment... no day but today!
Resolved, I take myself off autopilot, determined to make this next
trip around the sun in full life-force.
I take a deep breath, inhaling that perfect Spring night breeze, and
continue driving…
the Moon smiling at me the whole way home.

Valerie Leyden-Morffi
(Whiskey + Empathy)

SWEET DREAMS, BABY BOY

Back and forth, back and forth, back and forth.

I held you close as we snuggled in the new glider from Abuela, gently rocking...

Back and forth, back and forth, back and forth.

It was only our second night home, and I couldn't stop staring at you... you were beyond perfect – Those cheeks; beautiful, bright, dark-steel eyes; adorable little well-rounded chin... were you really mine???

A deep sigh escaped your perfectly pursed, pouty lips as if you too were in a state of nirvana.

I couldn't look away from your little hand, how it rested upon my half-exposed breast, tiny fingers spread wide... My heart melted and then swelled, an aching in my chest.

They don't prepare you for that feeling. Perhaps because there are no words to accurately convey the grandiosity of it. All I knew in that moment was everything that I am, was now You.

YOU are the love of my life, baby boy, and I promise to always be there for you, showing you every day how loved you are.

A small teardrop landed on your cheek, and you stirred. I didn't even realize I was crying. You wiggled some more, and I began to hum Brahms' 'Lullaby' as we rocked...

Back and forth, back and forth, back and forth.

The words started flowing from my lips to the tune; my own words…

Close your eyes.
Go to sleep.
Sweet dreams, baby Declan.
Mommy's here.
Always will be too;
B'cause I love you.

Day is done.
Time for rest.
All your worries away.
Close your eyes.
When you wake,
It'll be a brand-new day.

(And yes, that's correct… I've sung that song to you just about every night before bed since.)

I remember your breathing turned to the softest of snores then, and I smiled – the sound made me think of a tiny baby dragon.

You really were mine! And knowing exactly how blessed I was, I softly kissed the top of your head and continued on…

*Back and forth, back and forth, back and forth…

Valerie Leyden-Morffi
(Whiskey + Empathy)

KERI KASAME

AND HERE WE ARE

Pink on pink,
Me on you,
Together alone,
Alone together,
Trapped together,
In a cage of rhinestones and rubies,
A perfect shining exhibition,
Of pink on pink,
Me on you.

Keri Kasame

EMMA GLEDHILL

DESTINY'S SONG

My heart sings a song my beloved can hear.
It drifts on the breeze to draw him near.
He recognises my song as a match to his own.
Our hearts fit together, our destiny sown.

Emma Gledhill

A STORMY ESCAPE

Come find me my love and take me away.
I've need of peace, if just for a day.
My mind aches for rest, to find calm in the storm.
Let us hide for a while, away from the norm.

Emma Gledhill

MY ONE, MY LOVE

His love was an island amidst a turbulent ocean.
A sign of hope when none could be found.
A light for my darkness
The calm in my storm.
He was nothing but became my everything.

Emma Gledhill

WHITNEY REID

FALLING SWEETLY

I was eighteen during the ice storm of 2009. The treacherous roads could take you nowhere yet on a path of its own. If you dared to go, demise seemed to follow. It was a spiteful disruption that forced its sufferers into a solemn retreat. The wintry madness seemed to emulate my former years; cold and unkind. The snow would eventually melt and the sun would reign. I sparred with ice and battled fire, for summer had cinders that ignited hellish days. I fought endlessly to keep the ash at bay.

Even amongst the throes of punitive elements, I could find the inviolate beauty in a violent day. I figured love was the overwhelming warmth of dawn as it embraced the ice-glazed trees with a shimmer that glistened like gold. But to me, it felt like the crackling defeat of thawed timbers; filling the silent morning with the music of thundering echoes. I dreamed of the day when the summer would be kind and winter much nicer. In the wake of my dreams, came a lively display. The snow slept deep in the ground while flowers swayed. Then he appeared like a gentle breeze on an autumn day. I was suddenly fearful he'd be a season that wouldn't stay.

I hadn't uttered a word of needing love for love was something that had prickled and lanced. Love had been the ice daggers that hung upon sullen trees. Love had been the embers of a lustful touch that flickered in my heart and left with the rain. I yearned for something in between the angst of hot and cold; wherein I could flourish within an unprofaned scene. I needed something that would warm up the frost-bitten pieces that threatened to fall away and leave me broken and numb like the trees of that morning day. He inherently rustled within the shivers of my frosted heart and slowly, I melted.

With each passing moment, came a connection as deep as an ancient friendship; an unearthed bond. Maybe it was the lure of his smile and the light in his eyes. I freely eased into a heavenly place. His essence was as permeable as a sheath of mist and I was delightfully immured. Pieces of him whirled and separated within the fine breaks of gossamer sheen and enveloped me. We danced in the midst of the euphoric reveal and awaited the unseen.

Then with clarity and seraphic elation he held me close and answered my wish. He whispered an alluring envisage upon my ear, "you are stuck with me." So, then I leaned in for a fateful kiss. We later married where autumn met our divine union. The cold was held back and the sun gave off an aureate show. Nothing has since been too hot nor too cold. I'm enjoying the grandeur of Fall; falling sweetly amongst a thousand brilliant colors that paint my forever so wonderfully.

Whitney Reid

Give Me This Love

Give me the love that stirs so deep. I want to be lost where love runs free. Give me the light for the depths unseen; lighten the shadow side of me. So, give me the sun that awakens the night.

Give me the love that pulls you in and under, like a gentle wave or a shaded tree.

I want the way he dances to my restless heartbeat; give me more of this arcane harmony. I am shaken as he steals my breath with one kiss. I have no air left in my lungs, but only a song at the tip of my tongue. I let the melody loose as my lips fall in tune. I want your morning that guides me to another day and the dance that steals me away.

Give me more of this love- give me you.

      Whitney Reid

THE JOURNEY of LIGHT and LOVE FOREVER

I have two beautiful children that have given me the greatest journey to life and love. For that reason, I am able to delineate the unwavering power and beauty of such a bond. Assuredly, I can proclaim: Love is ever-present and permeates into the core of my heart and soul. Love is where I can be found. Love is where I'll never be lost.

Love is the teacher that leads me through the muddy waters of life, up to the highest point of the scenic mountain. I navigate the highs and lows of life and motherhood, knowing that the journey will be an altogether scenic beauty. I also believe the journey will never end because it's not supposed to. Love doesn't take one winding route and rest after an eventful excursion. That may be how the heart will journey when its beating tapers to an end but the soul has plenty of sights to see; love carries on.

How could I describe the way my journey to life and love began and will never end?...

I will begin with the miracle of my children, of which provoked the beat of my heart and immortality of my soul:

It's like the way a light enlivens a cold, dark room and spills through the curtains to make a dull place warm- how it transcends against all odds to make its way into your home.

It's like how their newborn eyes open and peer into yours as if they're resting on clouds and you control the wind. It's the way their tiny fingers grace and interlock with yours and you realize that touch isn't just a sense yet a miracle. Time passes and your demons shrink

to nothingness and fade as your soul catches fire and illuminates the godliness that exists wholly in every second of each day.

"Soul" isn't just a word, it's an everlasting journey. With that, I mean it when I say "I love you with all my heart and soul."

Then when you have experienced the fullness of light and love, you look back on the convoluted beings that tried to teach you the meaning and ways of love. The memories that were once a vivid dream of love fade into nevermore and become abstract and unrecognizable; the beautiful truth of what love really looks like is revealed and the macabre appearance of what was becoming a saddening apparition. You reflect on all that you thought was love and you see broken light that falls short of its flight and fades among the shadows; incomplete. How sad is it to have a beating heart and to be so broken that your love rests still among the darkness? How sad is it to have witnessed the birth of love and yet you have no light?

If there's one thing that I have made complete within myself and this life, it's love. I have light that leads me through the shadows and valleys. I have love that never rests among its journeys. My only fear is that my heart will stop to take a breath before my soul allows it. For this reason, it's the solace in a "Forever" that I take against my worries and shine upon my doubt.

So, to my children, I love you with all of my heart and soul- forever.

Whitney Reid

T H SMART

FIRST CAME the SHOES

Cinderella may have had glass slippers, but I had a pair of bubblegum pink bejeweled strappy heels. As I buckled the delicate strap at my ankle, I couldn't help but smile at the memory of the day I purchased them.

In need of some retail therapy, my best friend, Mary and I went in search of a much-coveted pair of heels. She had been eyeing them for some time, and with the seasonal sale having launched, we headed to the mall. If I had one weakness, it was definitely beautiful shoes. Imagine my glee when my first full-time job after completing my undergraduate studies was for a fashion shoe importer. I suspect my appointment was positively influenced by the fact that I had serendipitously worn a pair of heels they had imported and specially branded for one of their clients, a large local retailer.

It didn't matter that we were shopping primarily for Mary that day. I was just as buoyed by the prospect of getting our hands on her dream shoe as she was. Filled with optimism and hope, we strode excitedly towards our destination. On arriving at the store, we headed to the shoe department on the first floor. The sale shoes were lined up in the middle of the floor, grouped by size. Each size group consisted of two to three rows of shoeboxes, ten to fifteen boxes deep. The height of each stack was determined by the available stock. Each stack was crowned with a single shoe indicating the treasure beneath. While Mary searched for her shoe, I wandered over, without expectation, to the Size 5 stacks. A stiletto heel caught my attention. Bubblegum pink satin straps met sparkling pink jewels which crowned the instep before separating once more into a delicate ankle strap. I was smitten. At that moment, I knew this was no ordinary shoe. It was destined to transform its wearer into a princess. I gathered it up, and skipped over to Mary, confidently declaring I had found my wedding shoe. Despite my undeniably single status, my best friend's reaction was flawless. Without question or sign of doubt, she beamed back at me and bought into my fairytale notion. When the little voice in my head told me I was being ridiculous, Mary had my back. She knew what those shoes represented and was not going to let me give up hope that Mr. Right for Me did exist. Regardless of what the future held, I was not going to miss out on the perfect shoe. I walked out of the store with a sense of exhilaration. No one, other than my best friend, knew what was held inside the unassuming white shoebox I carried out that store.

Facing the second half of my twenties, I felt disillusioned and doubtful I would ever find the kind of love I had dreamt of and hoped for, and that was wrapped up in that beautiful pair of heels. I had picked up the shattered pieces of my heart too many times and was sure parts of it were lost forever. I did not know whether what was left was worth loving. What I know today, is that I first needed to find myself in me again. I needed to be ready to let go of the false identity I had come to believe - the one that said I was not worthy of lasting love. I needed to be my own Before Anyone Else to accept that I could really be another's.

I stopped searching for my Prince Charming. I hadn't stopped dreaming of wearing those perfect pink heels one day, I had just given myself permission to be enough on my own. And then, quite unexpectedly, I met my Before Anyone Else when he walked into my best friend's house and my life on a lazy Sunday afternoon. He had recently returned from abroad and popped in on the off chance that his childhood friend, my best friend Mary, still lived in the same house. That day was the start of a whirlwind romance just as my dad had predicted many months before. Several months later, one quiet Friday evening, he asked me to be his wife.

Five months later, I slipped my feet into my perfect bubblegum pink satin heels. I held my breath as I stood up and approached the mirror. My hair and make-up were done, and as I looked down I could see the clusters of pink silk blossoms adorning the iridescent white dress my mom had lovingly created for me. I looked into the mirror blinking at the princess bride reflected. One final touch would complete the picture I had held in my mind for the last few months. My mom slid the cathedral-length veil into my hair. I was ready for my perfect start. After all, I already had the perfect shoes.

T H Smart

THE SMILE

The owl called – I heard it.
Sad sullen shout heralding the night.
Darkness fell – I felt it.
Gently chasing after the sun's fading.
The crickets joined the meticulous chorus,
Sweetly serenading the sacred moon.
All fell silent as He reached out His hand
And lovingly caressed the tear-stained dunes.
One by one, the bashful stars
crept from their hiding place in the sky.
The stars sparkled – I saw them.
And as I looked up, I saw my Creator smile.
I closed my eyes and felt His blessing.

T H Smart

HIGH ON a NEW DAY

A heady sweet fragrance diffusing,
twisting, pulsating on the breeze of spring.
Intoxicating in a midsummer night's dream,
every creative who dares wade in the stream.
The mist, thick and tangible,
envelops every facet conceivable.
A sedative, satiating every ache and pain
dulling the hurt, as it starts to rain.

Splashes of splendor and waves of wonder
awake the heart from her deep slumber.
Awakened from what had been before
this mind created daze desires much more.

The warm, gentle kiss of the glorious dawn
lingering on the breath of the new sweet morn.
The promise of the secretive starlit night
transformed to the rapturous reality of daylight.

T H Smart

FIONA VAN ZYL

FOLLOW the TRAILS

Abelia was ready to leave. Her soul depended on her imminent departure. She had put all of her affairs in order, said goodbye to those who meant the most to her, and made her final preparations. To leave this world. To end her life.

Abelia had a fatal Illness: a cancer of the soul. It had taken root when she was still a youngster and it had grown throughout her teens, 20s, 30s, 40s. Now in her 50s, to defeat the illness that threatened her very soul, Abelia made the decision to die. Calmly and with precision.

This world had torn her to pieces. She shed fragments of herself everywhere she went.

Human Beings.

What are we?

Monsters.

Monsters masquerading as something superior. Pretending to be of the light while secretly feeding it to the darkness.

Abelia could not read another social media post about some unimaginable cruelty experienced by an innocent animal, inflicted by a human. She could not bear to hear the news apathetically reported about another disaster befalling the planet, a country, a person.

She just couldn't.

The horror of it all tore at her eyes. Her brain hurt all the time. Damaged by the effort it took to try and camouflage what she had seen, read, and experienced.

It was too much now.

The darkness had won.

Abelia packed the little she needed for this final trip. There was a bridge over a never-ending lake, tucked away in an almost untouched nature reserve. She planned to see it one more time. She would step off that bridge into the hereafter or the nothingness that may await us. Abelia was not sure what she believed. It didn't really matter. She just wanted out.

After an approximately three and a half hour journey, Abelia reached the outskirts of the reserve. Even its outer boundaries revealed it to be every bit as wondrous as she remembered. Everywhere she looked Nature was stretching out its limbs to touch the sky and connect with the earth. Mankind may have some presence here, but the humans are not in charge. Mother Earth and Father Sun are. Their union is a ubiquitous presence. The wind allowing seeds to hitch a ride on his back to set up house in another part of the reserve. To procreate, sustain and nourish. The sun playfully dipping and diving with the clouds; inseparable and indispensable to the natural world. Sentient beings clothed with feathers, fur, scales, gills, and more. All playing their part in the Great Cycle. No malice, just instinct abounds here.

Here Abelia felt truly alive. It was the perfect place for her to die.

She left her car somewhere near the entrance. She had no need to note exactly where; she was not coming back.

"Follow the Trails!"

An imperative echoed within the air as Abelia moved through the reserve.

She paused. Were there other hikers in the vicinity? She hadn't seen any, but who could she have heard through the canopy of trees and the footpath of dust? She brushed off her confusion and continued on her journey. Abelia inhaled every step of it, breathing in everything along the way as though to imprint it all onto her soul. She didn't want the horrors to be the only things living within its tissue and fibers.

She saw the bridge and the silvery depths flowing beneath. It was nearly time. Nearly time to pause the horror show that had been on repeat. She took a deep breath and stepped onto the bridge.

"Follow the Trails."

There it was again. Unmistakable. A little louder this time. Abelia could see no one else, yet she sensed she was not alone. Who or what was she hearing?

"It is I, the Wind." I not only breeze, blow and rage; I am a harbinger and I have a message for you.

Abelia of course assumed she had gone mad. Perhaps everyone about to greet their end has similar hallucinations.

"I am Wind. I am from this world, but not of it. I am physically here, but of spirit elsewhere. I come to move things; sometimes I am here to destroy things. Today I am here to pass something on. To you."

Abelia scoffed, now she was sure that she was mad. She had never mattered very much. She had never done anything important. Never been anyone of consequence. Why would the Wind be interested in speaking to her? And what message could he possibly have for her?

Wind began:

"First come the experiences and people that communicate we are not enough.

Next, we tell ourselves this, over and over.

It feels too hard and too lonely to go against the word of the world, so we repeat its often damaging message.

But the world is wrong. When it tells you that you are not enough, it is wrong.

It is an untruth coming from an ancient and wounded place. A place that is unable to see you.

A place that speaks an untruth because it is broken and sees and thinks and experiences in pieces.

But you are a whole. The sum of many exquisite, and yes, sometimes hurting parts.

But a whole. A total.

Do not listen to a slice, a chip, a bit that tells you that you are not enough. Even if this message comes from inside of you. Especially then.

You are a miracle. You are here, in this space and at this time.

Consider the probability of this and you will start to see, begin to recognise.

That you are important.

That you.

You.

You are an essential ingredient. You matter.

You do not need to listen to the pejoratives from a damaged piece.

You are a whole and You are magnificent!"

Abelia had no way of responding. She was aware of her resolve to die wavering, but she shut that doubt down.

"I am so appreciative that you have taken the time to speak to me Wind, your words mean more than I can express. But…"

"But you are determined to die."

"Yes, Wind. I am sorry but I am."

Wind shuddered almost imperceptibly. "Why are you so ready to throw away that which has been bequeathed to you?"

Abelia sighed. "I am sick Wind. What I have seen, what I have read and experienced. What many others have had to endure. The atrocities that have been dished out like after-dinner mints, as though the resultant suffering is of no consequence. As though those suffering do not matter. I want no more of it. It seems without end."

Wind paused.

Wind sobbed.

Wind shook himself and started to speak once more.

"You see only the dark. What happened to your sight?

You hear only screams. When did your ears lose their way?

You feel only despair. When did you abandon your faith?"

Abelia honestly did not know. She also did not know what to do about any of it.

"Look for the Trails."

They are out there. Everywhere.

Look for the Trails of Light. You have forged many yourself. Others have been left for you and for others."

Abelia still could not see. Not comprehend.

Wind reached into his pocket and pulled out a parchment. He unrolled it while never taking his eyes off Abelia, as though any blink may give her the opportunity to step off the bridge and out of this life. Something resembling a map started to emerge within the unfurling of the document. It contained what appeared to be a pattern of stars. The rising light: confounding and illuminating. Not pictures on paper but living constellations dancing with each other.

"Beautiful!" Abelia blurted out.

"It is you," replied Wind. "You and many who have crossed paths with you in this life, the ones before and those yet to come."

Wind knew how hard it would be for Abelia to access what he was about to share with her. Hard to process what she was really looking at. He would go slowly. Gently. He would introduce her to herself one step at a time.

In a place without time, Wind showed Abelia how she had created trails of light. When she checked up on a friend with a broken heart; when she cherished all the beautiful flaws in her partner; when she hurt so much she could hardly breathe, yet kept moving; when she loved so deeply the world stopped hurting for a series of moments; when she sang, wrote, dreamed. The snapshots Wind shared grew into a collage that grew into a constellation. Of Light. Hers and others. Merging and turning, ebbing, and flowing. Light healing dark corridors and dark shadowed corners.

Abelia started to see what Wind saw. What Mother Earth and Father Sun knew.

And she stepped off the bridge.

Not into the depths below, but onto the carpet provided by nature. She walked through the reserve and back to her car, back to the world, and back to her life. To find the light. To find herself.

She followed the trails of light and stepped into the All. The Everything.

Fiona Van Zyl

JENNIFER TORVALSON

A SAILOR MISLAID

The salt spray mingles with the sky
as I stand upon the misty shore,
the sea birds offer up their cry
to carry my sailor home.

Oh, sea who is my kin,
bear up my love to me -
rise up yon mighty waves,
crashing billows, issue my decree.

For amidst the pitching water
surely he doth sail,
his hand upon the helm,
his eyes searching o'er the rails,

mislaid amid the lonely deep
in want of his heart's home,
crusading the ocean's wiles,
seeking shelter from Aphros' storm.

For certain as the brine is vast,
reflecting barren as it is deep,
my sailor's spirit ebbs and flows
in tides of loneliness to me.

Oh, sea take hold the moon's beacon,
illume the murky grey,

that he might follow his soul's compass
and ne'er be spirited astray.

And I shall take my place here,
heart's flame beckoning to him,
on the fringes of thy noble waters,
my eyes upon the horizon.

And I shall make my vigil,
skirts borne up upon thy foam,
amidst the raging elements
til he is delivered safely home -

to these shores that promise him embrace,
and hands that hold the key,
to ancient destinies unfurled,
to a love born of the sea.

Jennifer Torvalson

JAY LONG

ETERNAL

One day
the bumps and bruises she so gently kissed away
will simply be scars
like bookmarks for the days of my childhood.

One day
the smile that lit the path each day will darken
and I will be left to find my way.

One day
the beat of my heart will be all that is left of her.

So I will cherish every moment
and savor each breath as they fill my lungs.

For a mother's love is eternal
and the life she gave me is meant to be lived

Jay Long

EVERYTHING

Step inside my mind and you will see
a window that looks out over all I know
all I hold close
all I cherish

Everything

My dreams
My fears
My loves
My missteps

Hidden from view are the victories
the battles I have won bless me alone
In the war I waged against an ordinary life
I have become my own beacon
My own saving grace

There are parts of me that are tarnished
I have left shattered pieces along my path
The vessel is dented and weathered
and when the last day finds me
The moments life tried it's best to break me
will forever remain ink stains on the page
So the world will know this man lived and loved

Jay Long

JODIE BENDER S.B.

MY GENTLEMAN

He is a gentleman.

He bridges himself across the muddied puddles of my memories so
that I may cross them with a clean conscience.
He jackets me with his embraces when the frigid voices of the past
have me shivering and frozen in place.

He stands up against my shadows when I enter a room fighting them
He firmly and steadily walks along the curb of my existence,
protecting me from the heavy traffic flow of ghostly memories.
He continues to open multitudinous escape doors for me,
every day carrying me across new thresholds
and securely closing the doors,
leaving my demons behind.

He is a true gentleman.

Jodie Bender S.B.

TIME of CIRCUMSTANCE

We were introduced by pure chance.
It felt like a homecoming in a greeting.
Our passionate first dance
was to a tune of circumstance.

It seemed more of a reunion than a first-time meeting.
A stranger and I with a history;
a foreign body I recognized immediately
as being a lifelong part of me.

Jodie Bender S.B.

WE ARE HUMAN

We are not all sunshine and rainbows,
nor beautiful poems and sweet prose,
Feelings do get hurt, and our voices do rise,
and occasionally pain slams our chests, and tears fill our eyes.

We work, and we struggle, and yes, sometimes we fight,
But we laugh, and we love, and we hold onto each other tight.

It's all about apologizing and compromising and prioritizing.
It's about passionately loving, sometimes falling, and always rising.

Jodie Bender S.B.

EMILY JAMES

FORGOTTEN LOVE

I'm not sure when it happened. I don't remember the day or the time or even how old I was. I don't remember when I stopped loving myself. Maybe I never actually did. Maybe it was something I never learned how to do. Oh, I knew how to love. I loved other people in my life. Some more than they deserved, but I think for so many years of my life I never even thought about giving myself even just a fraction of that love.

I think I figured out my worth from the way people seemed to love me. And from that, I thought I wasn't worth very much. So maybe that's it, I didn't think I was worth loving.

I walked a broken road for so long, never really sure where I was going. I kept meeting the same type of people. The body was different but the ugliness inside was always the same. And I mean that in all aspects of life. No one seemed real and I was just going through the motions. Day after day, it was always the same. The world seemed to drain me.

I had one bright spot in my life, my daughter. For her, I carried on.

One summer when I was in my early forties something in me broke. I was driving home from work, the day was beautiful. Sun was shining, windows were down and the music was loud. Out of nowhere, the tears started to flow. I knew right then and there I was changing. Why then? I have no idea. I finally admitted to myself that I was miserable and had been for some time. I knew I had so many things I needed and wanted to change. I had every right to be happy. I needed to start loving myself to have the life I truly wanted. A life filled with peace.

Who knew after years of not loving yourself that learning to do that would be so hard? I didn't. But every day is worth the struggle. I started to speak positively to myself and about myself. I started to do things I loved to do again, I picked up the pen again after years of not writing anything. I started to truly live. I forgot so much about myself getting lost in other people and had fun rediscovering all of it.

Every day I am continuing to learn to be the love of my own life…

Emily James

SAVANNAH STOVER, THE SCARLET WIDOW

NIGHT WHISPERS

You know that place between dusk and sunrise
That's where I love you
The secrets of night elucidate the brilliant hues of love
You're my favorite reason to lose sleep
Hushed confessions in our whisperings
Your face looking at mine
The subatomic pull brings us back each time

Savannah Stover

THE FIRE THAT MAKES US ALIVE

Love is inadequate a word
It is a fire that breaks and destroys
And builds and makes alive
I haven't met a cause for which living is greater
I'm filled with volcanic eruptions of affection
Of worshipful and tormenting love
Its red ribbon spirit has relentlessly pursued me in lives past
I drip with an unrealized intensity
It wakes me from my sleep
To taunt and tease
It demands, it hungers, it is insatiable in its quest
I know it wakes you in the night
Overtakes you with might
You fear even the sight
Of me, knowing it will leap
And soak you in my effervescent moonshine
Shaken, by love, a love you never dreamed of
I found you. I found you. I found you.
Let us take our fill, my love
To be destroyed by the wildfire descended from above
You cannot return to the place of the unseen
For now, you know of me
Need is too small a word
A wail from the altar of intensity is heard
Love has made her claim
She will not leave here ashamed

The rumbles of hunger seek their sate
It is to she whom we now belong
She grips us both in the name of fate
Perhaps it is the spirit of love that carries me through
This feeling of home that exists in you
The spirit transcends time and space
I ever seek after her face
In tormented need, I wait
For our fulfilled embrace

Savannah Stover

CHARLENE BENOIT

SAFE PLACE To LAND

We found each other on the darkest of nights,
When our wings had grown too tired to fly.
Heavy rain had been beating down on our backs,
So, we sought refuge away from the sky.

We had no intentions to get where we are,
We just knew we meant the other no harm,
And though we were both ragged and soaked to the bone,
Together we knew we'd keep warm.

As the moments of time passed between us,
We shared all of our secrets and fears.
Now, far from strangers, and much more than friends,
We've found a love that grows ever near.

So, I'll make to you this promise,
I will share my life and give you my hand.
You'll never have to face another storm by yourself…
I will always be your safe place to land.

Charlene Benoit

NEW RELIGION

It happens that way sometimes,
A love so deep,
The emotions exchanged,
Leave permanent marks.
Like cuneiform upon your soul.
Etched forever as sacred script
Across your entire being,
Changing everything
About your perception…
Nothing's left untouched.
As though you have witnessed
An ancient Sumerian deity
Scribe words meant
For your eyes only.
The foundation, a Holy text, from which
You'll build your new religion.

> Charlene Benoit
> William Hoeye

A LIGHT IN THE DARK

What makes you different from all of the rest?
I'm not sure if I have enough words to explain,
But there's something about you that's different than most,
And my heart flutters at the sound of your name.

There's mystery dancing in the dark of your eyes,
That hint that you know more than you'll tell,
They hold secrets of heaven and all of the angels,
And a survivor's long journey through hell.

Your voice has the power to both soothe and excite,
And travels deep down to my core,
Filling my thoughts and my dreams with new hopes
That we'll keep growing to one day be more.

Your smile, you know it's my weakness,
But in a way, I find new strength in it too,
It decays my defenses, leaving me open,
But those walls are only lowered for you.

You are a safe place where I don't have to be strong,
You let me be me and accept all my flaws.
You soothe and caress every scar and each wound
Left over from a time that once was.

You make me laugh, you make me smile,
You inspire growth and passion in me every day,
You don't make me question or worry what our future will hold,
You give me so many reasons to "stay".

What makes you different from all of the rest?
It's an unexplainable magic you do to my heart.
You are every answer to my every wish about love,
You are my fire, a light in the dark.

Charlene Benoit

ERI RHODES

SANDCASTLES

He pinned a piece of her scarlet hair up under her daisy crown and stared at her with star-struck eyes. "My beautiful Queen, don't you know you are a royal and regal warrior and a castle is where your heart belongs?".

She wiggled tattooed feet in the sand and threw her arms open wide. "My sweet knight, don't you know they don't just give castles to girls like me, with our dark hearts and our darker histories."

He smiled and his whole face danced along with his eyes as he began shaping a castle in the sand near the shore, just for her to let her hair down from. "Well, maybe we should start with sandcastles. We'll build them strong and fortified, like our love, so they never crumble and wash away. Then when we've finished conquering the world with our passion and this eager affection, when all hail the Pixie Queen, you may have your choice of castles".

She laughed at the somberness in his tone and she took his face in her hands so she could cover this face — the one that betrayed his every emotion, the features that both soothed and excited her —- She covered this face in kisses.

He always had a way that could draw her into any story, any fantasy, and make it seem like it was just sure to come true, no doubt, whatsoever. If he said she deserved castles, she believed him, even though her heart felt like a haunted castle all on its own. Ghosts of past loves, scars from betrayals gone by hanging like dusty cobwebs, and the pained memories of years of casual insults wandered the four chambers of her heart, declaring her unworthy. It was only here, in these moments seeing herself reflected in his love, and in her love for him, here with the love they proudly showed off to the world, that she felt worthy of even a fragile and easily cast aside sandcastle. Here, near the roaring infinite ocean, the eternal glow of the moon, and the sweet twinkling of stars - here holding him, holding her - here with fervent kisses cast across bare skin - here where he brings her to make her fairytales come true - here where he reminds her of their shared passions: mythology and music, promises, poems, and prose. Here he was the keeper of the words that unlocked her heart and she even didn't care if he meant them, as long as he kept repeating them.

Eri Rhodes

THE MULTI-WINGED BIRD

To Nathan Michael, the kid who made me a mom.
These words can't begin to capture the depth of your character.
No words can. But I tried.
Love, Mama

Dear Son,

First, you were my Little-Winged-Baby-Bird. All that I knew I
taught to you - How to live, eat, fly, and sing - To return to the nest if
ever the situation was dire. You grew up brave and strong and
gallant, soaring through treetops, far above lesser birds, but always
keeping mama bird, and her nest, in sight.

Then you grew into the Bigger-Winged-Bird and became a loving
and kind example to all the baby birds venturing cautiously from
their nests for the very first time. As if they could see the compassion
dripping from your lengthy, but harmless claws, into every single
thing you neared, they flocked to you, many times choosing you over
their Mama birds for comfort and wisdom. This Mama Bird's breast
swelled with pride.

Then with a blink of a bird's eye, you were suddenly the Biggest-
Winged-Bird. Loyal and responsible, and still sensitive and

honorable, you became the symbol for our family. You embodied the
timeless idea that you don't have to outgrow empathy and chivalry

and the love you have for your Mama Bird. Now when the weather turns colder and I feel as old as my grey feathers, I can count on your enormous wingspan to hold me through bitter winter nights. Our roles may have reversed with time, but in my heart, you'll always be the Littlest-Winged-Bird.

Eri Rhodes

MAKING PERFECT LOVE

He said my name, once, for the first time, and it was like no one had ever said it before. Did it always ring with the bells of angels or only when he said it while I drowned in his kind and sensual eyes? Did I even exist before he looked into my eyes and saw my soul for what it's worth? I know that love never looked as true as it did when our eyes locked for the first time, the second time, the thousandth time.

He touched my hand, once, and it was the first time anyone held it. Had I been touched before he ran his hands lovingly over every inch of the body I couldn't stand? Did my body swell and tremble and blush with pleasure before his hands first knew me? I know that neither I nor anyone else had ever loved my body the way he did, completely, as only a lover could.

He kissed my lips, once, gently pressing his mouth to mine. Had my pink lips ever parted with such thirst, such longing before calling his name? Had my voice ever strained with such excitation and elation before it met his as we joined together as one? I know now that two voices have never before made such a beautiful melody.

He reached for me, once, pulling me into an eager embrace. Had lust ever found a home like it found in the heat between our two racing hearts? Had love ever been made that shook the universe before our bodies rose and fell as one? I know now that when souls are meant to be, love can be made perfectly.

Eri Rhodes

C.N. GREER

TIME

Time knows no bounds
When we're together
Days, minutes, hours
They freeze in place
And go too fast, swirling
Together until time has
No meaning. I could have
Met you years ago or
Just yesterday and I would
Still love you the same
The seconds pound away
Bringing us together,
Binding our beings into
An essence that cannot
Be defined by the
Construct of a clock
We are limitless. And in
That freedom we have
Found the possibility
Of time

C.N. Greer

MEET ME THERE

Meet me there.
Somewhere between awake and asleep,
Where our dreams lead us in a dance among the stars.
Place your hand in mine, hold me against your chest,
Let me feel your heart beating in tune
As we escape our realities and give in to the beauty of midnight.
Hold me close as we count the lights,
The wishes kept safe in the inky black sky.
Walk with me through the winds that blow,
Let me feel your fingers in my hair as
The air swirls around us, our eyes shining,
Bright as the fires we feel within.
Take me away with a kiss that sweeps us up
Into the magic of the moment.
Let's lose ourselves in the maze of the unknown;
Explore the mysteries that live within our minds.
Lay with me as the hours pass us by,
Where the worries of the world slip away
Until there is nothing left but the wonders we've created.
Nothing but the two of us.
Meet me there.

C.N. Greer

COLORS

I see the world in colors.
For instance, he might be the darkest blue,
Like an ocean at midnight,
Still and calm, yet full of mystery.
But you...you are the deepest red of a brilliant sunset,
Just before it fades into the darkness of the night.
You are the horizon caught fire, so many
Vibrant colors swirling around to create a masterpiece,
All blended together until one bothers to see
Into your soul and can pick out each individual hue.
I see the world in colors, and you are more
Beautiful and dangerous than anything
I ever could have imagined.

C.N. Greer

AVANT AVANT-GARDE

BOOKMARKED

First time I ever fell in love, was with poetry
He was walking by, over 6ft
Artistry in motion
A beautiful novel-length of emotion
There was a quiet about the storm of his graces
And before I knew what had happened, I was lost in the pages
He spilled ink over the stages of my sighs
Made love to my innocence, line by line
Tore the edges off the paper of my soul
Taught me stanza could be sung—
And then retold

In a world of tyranny of smile
He was a book that created denial
If I had known, then,
what I know now
I would have kept that book—
like a crown

Every now and then I see my poetry
And I smile, as he smiles back at me
And I walk one way, as he another—
Humming the lyrics we wrote through covers

And I remember the beauty of his gentle
And how he treated my fragile like a temple

Paying homage, worship, and offerings
Teaching my senses words of Kings
Knowing he was the first to set me free
And in that, he will always be
And that is how I came to love—
poetry

Avant Avant-Garde

AMY JOY

A SONG FOR MY BROKEN "HEART CENTER"

A few years ago, I experienced a near-fatal car accident. It would require a lengthy hospital stay with an extensive recovery period.

My injuries were severe enough to include a fractured sternum among them. Less serious than an actual broken one, but painful nonetheless.

Ten days into my recuperation, I woke up to watch the sunrise through the window from my bed of the rehab hospital. I was graced with such lovely views since my room was on the third floor.

My still foggy brain settled on a Cat Steven's song about dawn breaking through the quiet morning. I hummed to the sun slowly bringing her dancing beam of light into my sacred space. Both music and nature had been instrumental to my healing and well-being.

My broken sternum protested movement as I attempted to nudge it awake with deep inhales that filled my belly, expanded my lungs, and raised my heart center. I had made my physical therapist laugh the day before at that term, "heart center." I was trying to explain where I felt the most pain and could not come up with a more clinical term.

My "heart center" has definitely been "broken" many times before the accident. I was no stranger to feeling poignant pain in the middle of my chest. I was used to inhaling through the intense throbbing that was intent on rendering me breathless.

I suddenly remembered a quote written by Isabel Gillies that read, "You find out what you are made of when you have a broken heart. If it happens early and often, all the better."

I believed that to be true. My "heart center" had been broken physically in the accident. Not long before that, it had been fiercely fractured emotionally and spiritually. And while those were some experiences I would have preferred not to have gone through, I was grateful for each and every one of them.

I discovered that my heart was built to be soft. My heart was built to be compassionate. My heart was built to be understanding. My heart was built to be strong.

I knew in that very moment my broken chest bone would heal. Otherwise, I would not have woken up on that Sunday so long ago with a song in my "heart center."

Amy Joy

DEBRA MAY SILVER

SLEEPING ON TOP

Sleeping on top of the covers.

But barely sleeping at all.

I have not done that for years.

Last time was when I flew across an ocean just to get my head
straight.

You said you were going to burn the house down your anger and
stonewalling was what I got.
Your memory was always marred and recalled what you told it
to......truth or not.

I dreamt of you for a solid week before running into you that day
Seeing you in our doctor's waiting room.
Talking to you I felt nothing, and just like my dreams I had little of
anything to really say.

Sleeping on top of the covers.
But barely sleeping at all

Sometimes I wonder if you have regrets.
Are you ashamed of your violent words and ripping walls and doors
apart?

My spirit was shattered into pointy shards for a while......... but you
never ever broke my heart.

Sleeping on top of the covers.
But barely sleeping at all

I can't regret a thing I gave it all, even though you never deserved my
half let alone my best
Cold hard Lessons I learnt I viewed it all like a third person from
above.

I never failed myself because I passed my toughest test.
Now I'm sleeping on top of the covers
But barely sleeping at all
And it's got nothing to do with you this time.

I'm sleeping on top of the covers and mostly feeling fine

Debra May Silver

SWIM ON

I've run out of things to say to you.
I think about that a lot and don't even have a sentence to explain it.

Sounds lame and empty but unfortunately it's true.
I just can't come up with anything that wouldn't be glib.

All the deep waters I felt for you
have somehow turned to a murky puddle.
I look to the sky for rain and see nothing but heat and blue.

I wonder if phony is the correct word
to describe our "apparent" connection.
We are a dime a dozen that's for certain.

I just can't come up with anything that matters to me right now.
My mind is doing all the work,
while my heart watches on with disinterested eyes.

You swam the roughest of seas and found a small island to rest on.
You've outgrown that place but insist on staying put.

I've enjoyed the beach and sunshine with you
But I need to swim on
Swim on

Debra May Silver

RUBY JANE PRIAS

WALK THROUGH

They say love conquers all, but I believe challenges enable them all. Trials and temptations taught me how two souls may connect and accept one another in order to avoid falling apart. Knowing you is both a test and an adventure. I am who I am today because of your love and support. They are the source of my happiness and resilience.

Everything I've learned has come through walking with you. Every success has its share of setbacks. Disappointments are a fundamental part of learning, and love requires trials in order to remain strong. Being with you made me who I am and what I am capable of. It also spurred me to think big and work diligently for them. You gave me hope and inspired me to achieve my goals.

rjprias

DADDY'S LOVE

Father, a loving figure who meets his children's needs while also acting as a guide for them. The one who will adore you no matter what. Someone who isn't constantly looking for flaws in you. The person who will always protect you and will never desert you. The only man who will never hurt you.

My father isn't perfect, but he is the best in the world. When everyone else has abandoned me, he is always there for me. When somebody insults me, my father is there to support me, get back on my feet and realize the truth. He treats me like a princess and guards me at all costs. He is willing to risk his life to save me. He is always willing to go to great lengths to make me happy.

He loves me with all of his heart, and I adore him a lot. No one can ever match his unwavering support for me. I know I'll always be his princess, and he'll always be my king, as well as my knight in shining armor. The only one who will not let me down and will continue to make me smile even on a gloomy day.

rjprias

NICOLE LABONTE

MY LIGHT

I have said it before; I was born into darkness, these clouds hanging over my head. Rays of sunshine peaked through, a tease for the storms that would follow. I was alone, even around others, I felt alone, I was alone.

No one held my hand that truly fed my soul, superficial like the wounds on my skin, my true scars hiding under the surface. For 27 years, I knew life only in the dark, trauma, grief, confusion.

The clouds finally parted when I held my baby in my arms, the daughter I always wanted, the one I loved unconditionally, unconditional love being something I had never known prior to her birth.

I watched her grow; as she learned to walk, learned to talk, meeting milestones, the warmth inside my heart only grew warmer.

When clouds tried to follow me, she was the light that blinded the dark, the sun that chased away the rain.

When my life changed drastically; grief so hard to hide, I wanted to run, wanted to hid, but she gave me the ambition I needed, to push, to keep going. To live.

I had never known my mother's love, but my daughter will always know mine. Selflessly, unconditionally, for every breath I take.

159

My true reason for living; my world, my best friend, my beautiful daughter. The brightest of light, in the darkest of times.

Nicole Labonte

LEIGH ALISON

HER ADDICTION

She thought she craved him
Like a junkie looking for her next fix
A high like no other with a hypodermic needle of Unconditional
Love, Understanding, and Acceptance mainlined through her veins
She thought she needed him
Like an alcoholic needs a morning eye-opener whiskey shot
A warming buzz like no other swallowed down with a surge of Peace
and Calm warming up her whole body
She thought she wanted him
Like a pill popper wants the medication that dulls a roaring mind
A numbing like no other that soothes the Restless and Numbs the
brain
She thought she loved him
Like a gambler loves the next big win
A hand of cards with their fate mapped out by the dealer of Life and
Love

But she was wrong

She craves him like a soul craves the truth
Honest words spoken despite the consequences
She needs him like the ocean needs the moon
An inseparable draw that controls the tides of Love and Lust as the
water meets the shore
She wants him like the moon wants the sun

In a perfectly balanced yin and yang of Light and Dark
She loves him like a tree loves the water
An irresistible draw quenching deeply parched roots

He is her lifeline
Her mainline
Her daily fix

And no matter how much time she gets to spend with him it still
never feels like it's enough

Leigh Alison

LOVE LINES

There's a line drawn in the sand
With the battered driftwood stick
of their Before and After YOU lives
It's invisible, this line
They can't see it
But they can sure feel it
It has been defined by every choice that either of them ever made
that led up to the beginning of their We, Us, and Our
It's the line that defines
how they know they will no longer tolerate
indifference or ingratitude, disrespect or disloyalty
It's the line that defines how they know
there is never any turning back
They crossed that invisible line in the sand hand-in-hand
and now they are inseparable
Bound together by the glorious ties that bind True Love
Now, if you look closely,
you can find them drawing their own lines in the sand
Lines of hope and healing, love and trust
Lines that create a beautiful mosaic of dreams and wishes come true
Lines that lead them to the center of their world
Lines that no matter how rough or stormy the Sea of Life gets,
cannot be washed away
Visible for the world to see
A road map of their hearts

And the directions of their journey
Together

Leigh Alison

FIRST LOVE

Lost and broken
In the midst of circumstances, she never dreamed she'd be in
Looking for love with all the wrong men
On the brink of giving up
Half believing True Love
Belonged only in the novels she could no longer read
Swipe right just one more time
One last chance
Just one more she vowed
Before she'd give up and find solace in her own company
Destined to be alone she thought
And then she met Him
The beginning of a whirlwind romance
With a man she no longer believed existed in today's world
Inseparable since the day they met
He swept her off her feet
And treated her with Love, Truth, Respect, and Appreciation
Even though he's her Last
He is her First True Love
The man who showed her what Love really is
And she knows
Without one doubt
That she saved the best for last

Leigh Alison

MOLLY ASTRID EGAN (MAE)

MY CAT JACK

He is running around while I am at school
My sister comes home and prepares a meal
that only he and his family will eat
He eats food with his brother and sister and adoptive father
I come home and go to bed,
he joins me later on,
his hair soft as I hold him close,
kissing the top of his head
He falls asleep in my lap while I watch a movie
I feel so much love for him

My cat Jack

M.A.E.

A LOVE THAT CAN NEVER BREAK

Sitting on a bench
A puppy in his lap
A German Shepard by her feet
The cool breeze swings her hair out of her face
And makes his cheeks rosy
They aren't looking at each other
They are staring at the falling snow as the sun begins to rise
The colors go from black and white to a rainbow
But all the while they are not looking at each other
They are cuddled together
They feel a warmth
But it is not because they are cuddled up
Or because of their jackets and hats
Or even because of the dogs
It is because of the fire that burns
The flickering flame inside of them
Their hearts
That keeps them warm
But it is not the kind of love that you or anyone is thinking
It is a friendship that will never die

M.A.E.

EVA COFFEY

MY ALLEGIANCE

To my King, I swear my allegiance
My heart, body, and soul are his
To do as he pleases
I submit to his pleasures
For he finds his joyful peace
Deep within my core

It may seem archaic to some
The way I commit to my beloved one
But this is how I truly love
The one who has given me his very all

There's no two ways about it
When you aim to forever own it
You've got nothing to lose
You can only just do
You love more and better
Heart is like a sponge
Absorbing love all around
Your soul finds ways
To give and to take
And you become light
As you dwell deeper into love
My King makes me his Queen
Of the Kingdom of all his hopes and dreams

Vowing fealty is such a small thing
When our love blossoms perpetually

Into the eternity of Heavenly spring

Eva Coffey

MY TRUTH

How can you be so sure of him?, they asked.

How?

Easy.

He fills up the holes in my heart.
He's a mirror to my soul in every way.
When he's near,
he brings me a deep-seated peace that I can feel
running through my veins.
When he's far,
I feel his feelings, his moods…
all of him in my very bones.
When I look at him, I can only feel love.
And overwhelming, never-ending, overflowing love
that warms the core of me.

That's how I know, for sure, that he's my one.
The only one and no other.

My absolute truth.

Eva Coffey

DIAMONDS IN YOUR LIFE

When you are at your lowest
And desperation hits you hard
Don't be surprised
When people that you love
Leave you

Don't begrudge them
For not being able to be there
For you

Forgive them
For their weakness
And cherish
The good memories
For their time with you
Has come to an end
Send them love
Wish them well

But
For those who choose to stay
Who simply love and give support
Who holds your hand and be your guide
Whose beliefs and faith in you never waver
No matter what

Don't neglect them
Don't forget them

Appreciate them
Show them your respect
And treasure them

For they are
The diamonds in your life
Love them with everything that you have
Your life will be richer than you could ever imagine

They are the ones who will help you to fly high
The ones that will help you to reach
The highest castle in the sky

Eva Coffey

ELIZABETH

WALK WITH ME

Walk with me and drop your lines
I want to hear all about your life
Your joys, your sadness
Your naive teenage madness
Who was your first, and why did you fall?
Did you ever feel like you'd lost it all?

Walk with me, your hand in mine
Remind me how we lived our lives
Our laughter and tears
Our strength through fears
Who held who when we were weak?
Whose love screamed louder when we didn't speak?

Walk with me, please don't go
I don't think I can do this alone
My heart is breaking apart in two
Carry your half of me with you
Will you wait for me on the other side?

Always, until then,
The love of your life

elizabeth

PAPA

An innocent gaze of glorious surprise,
a world of wonder through a child's eyes
Come play with me Papa, hurry come see
I'm running quickly - will you follow me?

I have so much to show and tell
I made this for you…colored it myself
Just because you can never have enough
A picture of me and you
with a yellow sun on a sky so blue

Papa, Papa you're finally here!
I've waited all day so I could share
I learned to count and sing my ABCs
Oh, come sit down and have some tea
Please read me this story one more time,
I like your silly voices instead of mine

Your tickles, your hugs, your slobbery kisses…
all the things I cannot resist
Your smiles, your laughter, your outstretched arms…
are just what I need to fill up my heart
Cherished moments and dreaded good-byes
You are my world in Grandpa's eyes

elizabeth

WOULD YOU LET ME?

Would you let me...
Want you, delicately in the absence of light
With a desire that swells over time and
returns deeper than any ocean's divide

Would you let me...
Touch you, deeply beyond your bones
With sweet kisses and soulful stories
intricately woven across your golden canvas
and in places unknown

Would you let me...
Hold you, passionately in between our words and time spent
With memories tightly folded around our hearts,
armed with cherished intent

Would you let me...
Love you, more than you love yourself
With admiration for your strength,
forgiveness for your mistakes,
compassion for your sorrows,
and a devotion for all that you are worth

I'm here.
Would you let me in?

elizabeth

KCL WORDS

IF YOU FORGET ME STILL

if you wake one morning with hands
that have forgotten me, do not wonder
why your fingers ache for soft petals.
just recline in flush fields, your weight
crushing blooms between the curve of hills
and let your mind wander as to why they
gasp in familiar velvet tones

if you lie awake at night, hungry
with lips that have forgotten me, do not
question your craving for ripened fruit
fill your mouth, gluttoned with their
pink honeyed flesh, letting your tongue
dart out to capture the trails that drip
down your chin as my lips fill your mind

if days find your soul is restless in forgetting me
drink red wine by the sea, letting the tide lap at your skin
and read poetry to the forest, your words as Neruda,
touching each maple and pine and fern, letting
the earth whisper back with my name

if you forget me, if you forget me still
and find yourself lost to the world
listen to quivering sighs on the breeze and the ardent
cries of a thunderstorm; to the way the moon and

constellations give meter to your heart without reason
and let me find my way back to you, my love

kcl_words

SLOW DOWN

i love you but i need to slow down

 and by slow down, i don't mean
love you less, i mean...savor

 i love you but i need to slow down rushing through the want as
it fills me, filling me
filling me
overflowing me
leaving me gasping for breath, my hands frantically reaching for
anything to grab a hold of before i drown...but i want to drown

 i love you but i want to slow down the fear
that loving you will kill me, i want to stop fighting
this storm of my own making and let it overtake me
let me learn to breathe in the water, letting my lungs fill with you

 i love you but i want to slow down the beating in my chest
so loud i miss the words you say without speaking
let me instead hear the symphony between each contraction of
my heart, your heart...our hearts
let me feel the sway of blood carried by each note, the sway of blood
that sings when you are close, the sway of blood when you whisper
my name with the reverence of a thousand lifetimes

i love you but i need to slow down...and we could give in to
the urgency that leaves us gasping for air and filled with missing
days but instead i will fill a thousand nights with the
shape of your lips, the feel of your lips...the taste of your lips

then a thousand more with the smell of your skin
at the hollow of your neck and the way it tightens across
your chest, your arms, your thighs when i touch you

 i love you but i need to slow down and love you better ...deeper...
with a trust that i don't need to rush this love because
it is mine, it is yours,

 it is ours

 and we have an eternity to enjoy it

kcl_words

MERCY

he calls me mercy
his hand casually
running across
the warm sensitive skin
at the low of my back
sun from the open
sheer white curtains
spilling into the room
calls to morning

we lay naked on
now crumpled sheets
and discuss the day
contemplating lazy
exploration as i sip
the ginger tea he's made
from my favorite cup
painted in delicate
forget-me-nots

my eyes closing to
pleasure at the spice
on my tongue and
the touch now intently
traveling across the
curve above my thighs
his low voice in harmony
with the waves kissing
the beach just outside

slowly moving the tea to
the table next to the bed
(pale well-grained wood, knotted
and trimmed in ocean turquoise)
i turn to him, my lips softly|
cutting off his words
and gather every tender
ardent passion this man
holds in devotion to me

he calls me mercy
but he is mine

kcl_words

LORNA HUSBAND

PIECES of YOU

The pieces of a life that never die
a lock of hair, your lipstick and perfume
I inhale deeply and for just a moment you're still here
I play your favorite songs and can still hear you singing
I hang the special Christmas ornament each year remembering what
you said

      "here's something to remember me by"

as if I could ever forget you
you were my person
the one person that touched my life like no other
you were always afraid you'd be forgotten
I hope you know I will always remember
and those pieces of you, live on in me

      Lorna Husband

BREATHTAKING

He stood at the altar in front of God, family and friends
nervously sweating, shifting his weight
about to be wed to the love of his life

Finally, the moment arrived, as the first notes played
everyone stood and turned to catch a glimpse of his bride
she was so breathtakingly beautiful, just like an angel

His breath caught in his throat; his eyes glistened with tears
he felt the love all around them as they joined hands
this woman, this vision, now to be his wife

Lorna Husband

LOVED

I never knew just how good it all could be
until that day when you said you loved me
you accepted me as I was, never seeing a flaw
you always looked at me with such wonder and awe
I never grew tired of seeing that look in your eyes
your touch always gave me chills that brought sighs
in your arms I felt complete, like an all-natural woman
you always reminded me you were proud to be my man
and for the first time in my life, I was loved for me
until that day, I never knew what it felt like to be free

Lorna Husband

SHAUNA WOODBURY

ALWAYS IN ALL WAYS

If it pleases you,
A midnight walk
If it eases you,
A light breezy talk
If it sparks your fire
If it takes you higher
There are things said and done after dark
A song only we share
A hearts dance of endless care
Some regret and some satisfaction
Some sweat and some salty action
Some pleasure and pain.
Days of sun.
Nights of sultry steam and rain.
We will hold hands and talk of days gone by
We will stop by your parents stone for one last goodbye
We will sit with our faces to the sun
We will live this life as one
Rocking chairs and grand-babies someday
If it pleases you, will you take me forever on this day?

Shauna Woodbury

ME and MY FREE

There's sunshine in my morning with coffee by the water's edge.
There's whitecaps on stiff fresh ocean mist.
The warm air clean and free.
I am me.
Easy-rolling moments, not wasted days.
There's wine in my afternoon by the gravel road gate.
Green hills rise to the sky
and clouds dance in the left forward winds.
Peaceful thoughts.
Free to be me.
There's warm food by the fire's light and reflection of my joy,
the tranquility that gives comfort to my scene.
I'm free to be me.
There's soft linen off the floor by a white velvet moon as I lay to
sleep.
Midnight brings dreams and the stars wave goodbye
to give life of a new morning with sunshine by the water's edge.
Free to be me.

Shauna Woodbury

VALERIE MESTA

RABBIT'S HOLE

I love you with the fairy tale love
I thought would never exist for me…
You chose me when I chose you,
and now we're holding hands jumping into Rabbit's hole willingly.
We're looking forward to new adventures fearlessly
with passion in our eyes and love in our hearts.

This is the part where we can be happy
or reign any place we go as long as we're together.
This feeling is fucken amazing,
and the only fear we have is losing each other.

I didn't believe in a love like this for me…
And now you are my happily ever after.

Valerie Mesta (Take Me To the Trees)

RAYNE

He saved my life.
I was drowning.
I was getting ready to follow the crowd…
And he saved me.
Drugs were in reach
and my strength began to read as a boring weakness.
I almost became a follower.
I almost became fun.
I was almost tempted to hide my pain just like everyone else,
but he saved me.

As he grew in my belly I knew I had a greater purpose.
Even at the age of fifteen I knew my job was to protect him.
I was a child expecting a baby and he was life in every way.
He saved me from mistakes and the path that was expected of me.
Yes, I would be a teen mom,
but I would never journey the path generations before me had.
My son Rayne saved me before he was born
and now my four children continue to breath life into my lungs daily.

I have purpose.

I have hope.

I have love and it all started with Rayne.

Valerie Mesta (Take Me To the Trees)

FOUND BY STRANGERS

I fell like a shooting star falling onto uncharted land.
I was small, broken, and worthless.

My heart beat was faint,
and I found myself hating the fact that it was beating at all.
I was ready to give up,
but with blood as ink I began to tap my truth onto a screen
with words so raw it revealed my pain.
Liquid salt rained, and Liquid salt reigned.

I felt a slight feeling of relief as I tapped the option to post
and read my own words back to myself.
I said shit I was taught to hide…
I was doing something that was frowned upon,
and I watched people who knew me ignore my pain.

I was nothing…

I was nothing until

I became something more than inferior in the eyes of strangers.

They called me brave and thanked me for the truth
and the rawness of my words.
They made me feel human.
I finally had a voice and I wasn't invisible.
It was fucken beautiful in the deepest way.
Broken things became art.
Broken things became mosaics…

I wasn't worthless and neither were they.

We were simply humans being challenged and learning lessons.
We were warriors and now we knew it.

Screen tapping, liquid salt, and a bit of cursing
brought light in the dark and warmth to the soul.

Screen tapping and identifying took me to the trees.

I was free.

I was alive.

I was strong and I was fucken art!

Valerie Mesta (Take Me To the Trees)

MICHELLE SCHAPER

FIRES OF HUMANITY

Leave a light on
in your heart
the light of your own soul
to guide
the lost ones
through the dark
like a burning
candle of poetry

When you open
your heart
to see
with non-judgemental eyes
compassion will burn
from your flames
through the fires
of humanity.

Michelle Schaper

HEART STRINGS

I think the whole world
is the spine of something bigger
and we are but the little bones
holding it together
We need to make connections
so it doesn't fall apart
or maybe we're the strings
and the whole world
is a pulsing heart

Michelle Schaper

WHISKEY ANGELS and WINGS of INK

This goes out to those
with the flamed whiskey souls
who feel passion burn
through their blood, a yearn
The longing to be
something wild and carefree
but they're caged in their thoughts
a prison of sorts
So for you they will bring
spilled ink to sing
their reflections of mind
sometimes sad, mostly kind
Giving words a sweet cadence
rhythmical decadence
connecting through shared sorrows
or dreaming of our tomorrows
Uniting us all
with each rise and fall
the dreamers, ones called 'a poet'
softening the madness
of life as we know it

Michelle Schaper

ABOUT THE AUTHORS

MICHELE SCHAPER

Michelle Schaper, from Western Australia, works as a support worker/carer for disabilities, (or as she says, 'enhancing people's abilities.') She is a mentor/advocate for mental health and domestic violence and has written poetry since her childhood. You'll find more of Michelle's work on Facebook at facebook.com/chellessoulpoems and @michellesoulkissing on Instagram. Her books 'Soul Kissing' and 'Fairytale Bones' can be found at some online bookstores.

MARGIE WATTS

Margie grew up in the Eastern Coastal area part of Georgia known as the Golden Isles. She loved it there, living near the ocean. Even as a child she loved looking out past the horizon. It felt like looking at forever. Walking, sand between her toes and picking up seashells. Just her and her shadow. "Me time", she called it. Butterflies was another of her favorites. Their beauty as they flew around. How they start out in the darkness of a cocoon and find their way out into the light as a beautiful butterfly. A reminder that darkness is not always a bad thing. There can be beauty from darkness. She was always an avid reader and a constant dreamer. Her debut book Wounded Butterfly was released in 2020. Her follow up book, Reflections of Me is now available as well, via the Amazon worldwide marketplace. Follow her on Facebook at facebook.com/reflectionsofawoundedbutterfly

SHAUNA WOODBURY

Shauna was born in Calgary Alberta Canada. She writes, plays baseball, loves beer and festivals. She writes from a darker side but loves the rainbow fireworks the little happy moments in life bring. She has two sons and a beautiful life partner to complete her world. Her future endeavours hope to include more writing, more living, and brighter connections. At the age of 50 her life and literary creations are just beginning. Join her on her journey. https://www.facebook.com/SexLeatherHearts

NICOLE LABONTE

Nicole Labonte is a single mom to one daughter, and a 15 year old cat. She lives in a small city in Ontario Canada.   She is a poet, but loves writing short stories. In August of 2020 she self published her first novel, the first of a trilogy, a modern-day fantasy fiction novel titled "The Wand."   Nicole loves music, mostly of the post hardcore genre, enjoys playing piano and a lover of live (rock) music.   Nicole is a dedicated mom, and a loyal aunt, sister and friend. She has many nieces and nephews that are loved as her own children, and friends who are loved as family. Nicole works full time in the cosmetic industry, and uses her off time to write as much as possible. She started writing at ten years old, and has only continued to find her passion through writing what is in her soul.

TAKE ME TO THE TREES

Valerie Mesta (Take Me To the Trees) considers herself an amateur writer who uses poetry as an outlet for emotional trauma left by the many abuses she experienced through her life. Her story began before she could remember, and includes molestation, physical and mental abuse and rape. She often refers to the people who abused her as monsters in her writing, and considers herself a warrior, not a survivor, because she's still fighting the demons of her past in her head. Valerie suffers from PTSD, Bipolar, Anxiety, and Depression which comes through in her writing. While she often calls herself worthless, she believes that she's strong even in her weakest moment. Valerie shares raw words honestly as a form of therapy. She also believes identifying is comforting, and key to helping others with similar issues simply feel human. She says writing is her only voice, and her screaming into a pillow is ranting online. You can follow her online at facebook.com/JustTakeMeToTheTrees and instagram.com/take_me_to_the.trees

EVA COFFEY

Eva Coffey, a cheesy romantic coffee lover, always has an obsession with words. She

writes from her heart about things that matter like faith and love. While grief is a lonely dark place, she hopes her words can offer some kind of solace to the ones who need them. She can be found at coffeylovenook.com | facebook.com/coffeylovenook

ELIZABETH

Howling Wolf Poetry is penned by elizabeth. The daughter of a self-proclaimed Grammar Queen and an artistic outdoorsman known for his watercolor paintings, elizabeth has been writing poetry for over 30 years – unbeknownst to most people in her life – until now. She has artists of different mediums on both sides of her family; some incredibly famous, and some just really good at what they do. With encouragement found in online writing and poetry groups, she began to reveal what only she had known – parts of herself and others in words of Life, Love, Loss, and Lust. Born and raised in California between the mountains and the ocean, she spends as much time caressing the earth as she does the keyboard. Her tolerance is high, her temper is low, and her love of animals and people is wider than any compass can measure. Follow her
facebook.com/howlingwolfpoetry | instagram.com/hwlgwlf_poetry

C. HAGE

C. Hage is a Nebraska native trying to bring light to sex, marriage, mental health, and self love. She writes about past trauma and real life experiences focusing on topics that tend to make people uncomfortable and push some of the normal boundaries. You can follow her at instagram.com/writer.c.hage/ and facebook.com/CHage-113914640020522

JENNIFER JENNINGS DAVES

A relative newcomer, Jennifer Jennings Daves is finding her place in the world of social media writers. However, she is not limiting her capabilities and is working to stretch her talents to the farthest reaches. Jennifer's writing is as often playful as it is brutal. Two sides of a completely complex and beautiful soul - one that invites you into the garden for tea but warns you of the dangers of sitting too close to the rose bushes, as she plucks the bloody thorns from her heart, one by one, and offers them to you. Whether it is prose, poetry or a song, she will definitely capture your attention as she serves up delicate pieces of her soul. Follow her iworeabraforthis.com | facebook.com/snapandflingitoff

C.N. GREER

Growing up in the Pacific Northwest, C.N. Greer has never been lacking in inspiration. In the last twenty years, she has taken that inspiration and expressed it for the world through the written word. An avid book reader, C.N. Greer is a fantasy writer and a poet. She hopes to share that love of fiction with her daughter. When she's not writing, she's spending time with her family and wrangling the fur babies that keep her life interesting. She believes in the human spirit and a person's capacity for strength and resilience, but she also knows those virtues can be hard won. She is an advocate for equality and compassion, and she hopes to bring some light into this world with her work of poetry and prose.

NICOLE CARLYON

Nicole Carlyon is a sensitive soul, a day dreamer, dabbling in random words as a form of escape from a past that eludes her. She writes to help herself heal, and hope that in doing so she can touch others and make them feel less alone in a world that doesn't always make sense. Raw and real the words that flow come from Nicole's soul and she does not apologise for being who she is (although she is still on a journey to find out who she is). Nicole's promised herself that she will keep writing until she find her true self or until the words run dry and she has nothing left to give. You can find her at instagram.com/nicolecarylon , facebook.com/HerDestinyDreamsandDesires and facebook.com/freetobesoulsensitive

LORNA HUSBAND

Lorna is an avid reader, bibliophile, devoted cat mom and nature lover. Born and raised in the Great Lake State, she is drawn to water and enjoys the changing seasons. As an amateur photographer, wildlife and natural landscapes are her favorite subject matter. She began writing for personal pleasure at the age of ten, but after college the creative urge was pushed aside while pursuing other goals. In recent years she has found the urge to pick up the pen again and she believes everyone has at least one good poem in them if they can listen to their heart and let the words flow. You can follow Lorna at instagram.com/bridgesnotburnt

KCL_WORDS

Kim LaSusa, 50, (kcl_words) lives in New York and is the mom of two humans, two cats and a dog that won't stop barking. She works in finance by day, spending her free time in her garden and writing under the pen name kcl_words. A free verse poet with the need to capture emotion, Kim hopes to keep sharing her words with others. You can find her on Instagram (www.instagram.com/kcl_words) and Facebook (www.facebook.com/iamkclwords)

D.B. WRIGHT

D.B. Wright resides in England, but his heart and soul belong to Ireland. A loving husband and father with a passion for words in all forms. Outside of writing he finds solace and joy in his family and friends, movies, and thoughts of travel. He is committed advocate and ambassador for mental health, working on a volunteer basis to support people with their battles, having battled his own traumas and demons his whole life. Follow him at instagram.com/d.b.writes and facebook.com/dannyboywrites

KATHY A. TATAY

Kathy A. Tatay was born and raised in Dallas, Texas. Her writing reveals many of her life experiences as well as her love of nature. Poetry, rhyming and words are her first love. Her quest in life is Spiritual Enlightenment and personal healing. Kathy has one published book, "Kaleidoscope Heart" and a poetry page on Facebook at facebook.com/PoetryofKatt and Instagram at instagram.com/Kattpoetry.

KELLI J GAVIN

Kelli J Gavin of Carver, Minnesota is a Writer, Editor, Blogger and Professional Organizer. With over 400 short stories and poems published and posted online, her work can be found with Clarendon House Publications, Sweetycat Press, Linden Books, The Ugly Writers, Zombie Pirates Publishing, Setu, 300 South Media Group, The Story Pub, Cut 19, Humans of Love, Otherwise Engaged, Flora Fiction, Margins Magazine, The Basil O'Flaherty, The Rye Whiskey Review, Some Good News, Sweatpants and Coffee, and Southwest Media among many others. Kelli's first two books were released in 2019 ("I Regret Nothing- A Collection of Poetry and Prose" and "My Name is Zach- A Teenage Perspective on Autism"). She has co-authored over 25 anthology books. "Stories I Should Have Written" will be published in 2022. She is currently writing a collection of fiction short stories.

Check her out at www.kellijgavin.blogspot.com @KelliJGavin on Twitter, Instagram and Facebook

JOHN SWEIGERT

As I sit down to write, my motive is as clear as it has always been. I want to write something so that people can relate and in so doing, be free to explore, dream and believe. This is just an opinion, and my thoughts and ideas are just that....thoughts and ideas. Believe in yourself, sprout your wings and fly.

Follow John at facebook.com/sweigertscribblings

BRIAN BERRYMAN

Brian Berryman was born in Abington Massachusetts, and currently lives in nearby Bridgewater. A former auto mechanic who transitioned to IT almost twenty years ago, he works in IT support for a community health care center in Boston. When he is not writing, Brian enjoys spending time with his fiancée Leigh and her two sons, playing guitar, singing karaoke, British sit-coms, and exploring Antique Stores. If you would like to check out more of Brian's writing, you can find it here;
https://www.facebook.com/FlameLilyPoetry and
https://www.instagram.com/flamelilypoetry/

CHARLENE FOX

Charlene Fox was born and raised in a suburb south of Detroit Michigan. Of five daughters, Charlene was the artistic one who loved crafts, painting and poetry. She started writing as a hobby in high school and continues to write many forms of poetry and prose. Charlene loves animals and had fostered rabbits and guinea pigs for the Michigan Humane Society for several years. Charlene still resides in her hometown with her rescue cat Halfpint. To read more of her writing you can find her on Facebook at
facebook.com/charlenesclosetofthoughts.

TRACEY KOEHLER

Tracey Koehler is the single mother of three beautiful children who worked multiple jobs while attending university to support her family. Ink had always filled her veins, but she had little time or energy to put words to paper. Life had been hard for her as she lives with a chronic medical disorder and suffers from PTSD and bipolar depression due to long-term abuse. After 25 years of silence, she gained the courage to pick up her pen once again to share her stories through poetry. Her first book, Beautiful Chaos: Learning to Live, can be found on Amazon. She is a small-town Indiana girl sharing the chaotic reflections of her heart and soul. Through her writing, she hopes to inspire others and give them the courage and strength to live their best life and fulfill their dreams, regardless of their challenges.

Her work can be found at:
https://www.facebook.com/Kissesfrombloodstainedlips

VICTORIA CORBETT

Victoria Corbett is a resident of South Carolina and a mother of two boys. Writing poetry is a hobby she has dabbled in for over 35 years. She started writing to connect with others through the heart. She has been voted fan favorite in her works of erotica and romance on a couple different platforms. She hopes to one day self-publish her own book.

ANN MARIE ELEAZER

Ann Marie Eleazer, author of She's Magic & Midnight Lace, as well as contributor to As Darkness Falls, is a writer of all things darkly enchanted, with a few spells thrown in along the way. A bit otherworldly herself and in her writing, she hopes to take her readers on enchanted flights through fairy tales and magical places...places where we often find our inner light and true selves. You can find more of her writing at facebook.com/shesmagicandmidnightlace and instagram.com/shesmagicandmidnightlace_/ Her book She's Magic & Midnight Lace is available worldwide via online booksellers.Ann Marie Eleazer, author of She's Magic & Midnight Lace, as well as contributor to As Darkness Falls, is a writer of all things darkly enchanted, with a few spells thrown in along the way. A bit otherworldly herself and in her writing, she hopes to take her readers on enchanted flights through fairy tales and magical places...places where we often find our inner light and true selves. You can find more of her writing at facebook.com/shesmagicandmidnightlace and instagram.com/shesmagicandmidnightlace_/ Her book She's Magic & Midnight Lace is available worldwide via online booksellers.

RUBY JANE PRIAS

Ruby Jane Prias (rjprias) is a Physics Teacher that loves to introduce different ideas on how young learners will enjoy learning. Born and raised to appreciate everything in life. She loves to write in every situation that she's in, every feeling that she has. She usually spends her free time writing to express her emotions. You can find her at facebook.com/creativelybroken | instagram.com/gracefullybrokenjdg

GYPSY'S REVERIE

Gypsy's Reverie is a woman who considers herself to be a free spirit, wandering far off the beaten path and following her wild heart in relentless pursuit of passion and an authentic life. Her writing tells the tale of her struggle to climb out of the dark abyss and back into the light--finding her truth and herself again after years of feeling broken and lost. Always a lover of words and stories, she began writing to help herself heal and to chronicle her process of becoming. The pursuit of authentic connections and relationships with herself and others is one of her top priorities. Gypsy's Reverie is so thankful to be able to share her journey on the road less traveled with other wandering souls through her words. It is her hope that her writing may serve to encourage, inspire, and/or amuse you while you travel through this life. Follow her at facebook.com/ascended.from.ashes and instagram.com/gypsysreverie/

DEBRA MAY SILVER

Debra May Silver is an established poet and editor. She is founder of Ship Street Poetry and author of "My Rabid Fucking Soul." Her poems have been featured in "The Frances Anthology" Australia and "Rise from Within" by 300 South Media Group New York.

Her style is more often modern, raw and dark which is reflected in her writing and black & white photography.

Visit her website www.debramaysilver.com or on instagram at: instagram.com/debra_may5 | instagram.com/shipstreetpoetry/

AVANT AVANT-GARDE

Avant Avant-garde is a profuse lover of words—words, the saving grace and the hellfire of how she draws breath; the only spoken her soul is literate in. Inspired at an early age by the Classic poets that have paved the way for us to embrace calligraphy of the soul, her page, Avant-Avant-garde, and several others I write for-- Black & Gold Poetry Page etc... are dedicated to being an advocate for writers of all levels across various social media platforms and published work. Follow her writing at facebook.com/SavantAvantGarde and look for her upcoming book, Forged In Ink coming out this Spring.

D. RODGERS

D. Rodgers, aka Plucky Em, has been through a lot these past few years, but she has never has given up her fighting spirit. She is currently living in one of the most beautiful mountain states in the US. Her home is filled with many children, including two furbabies. From an early age, she has always had a love for writing. She is an accomplished poet, hoping to publish her own works in the near future, taking others on her healing journey through poetry. It is her desire that her writing will touch readers who have survived trauma, giving them hope and healing, as she has found. You can follow her at facebook.com/PluckyEm and instagram.com/thewritingsofpluckyem/

SHAWNA OLIBAMOYO

Shawna Olibamoyo has dabbled in writing from an early age but it wasn't until 2014 that her poetry really came to life. It was a very challenging year which included a partial amputation of her right leg. As the words poured out, they became her escape and her therapy. Shawna really enjoys writing poetry and being able to express herself with every heartfelt word whether it be of love, pain or inspiration.

Without the words, there is no light.
Without light, we cannot find our way.

Find Shawna on Facebook at facebook.com/poeticblueprints

APRIL Y SPELLMEYER

April Y Spellmeyer began to write when she lost her husband in 2011. When April penned her first piece of poetry the floodgates opened up about loss, grief, mental illness, and trauma. While April expresses in raw, unfiltered emotional imagery she balances it with the beauty of hope, love, strength, and healing. April finds several genres of music bring her words to life to tattoo them on the world. April is a mother to four children, three fur babies, and Gigi to three grandsons. April enjoys reading, history, Star Wars, and enjoying time with her family. April is the author of Sacrifice & Bloom, Scars of a Warrior, and Poetry Stained Lips. In the Fall of 2022 Graffitied Bones will be released. You can find her books on Amazon and follow her on Facebook at April Y Spellmeyer - Author facebook.com/AprilYSpellmeyer and on Instagram at Eternal Soul Sisters instagram.com/EternalSoulSisters.

LYSSA DAMON

Lyssa Damon lives in Cape Town, South Africa, in the heart of the winelands with her family and assortment of weird and wonderful pets. Lyssa has written in some form or another since she can remember, starting with a poem about kittens losing mittens in a puddle. She dabbles in poetry, short stories, flash fiction and is attemptong to write a novel. She dreams of one day turning at least some of those stories into a screenplays. Lyssa loves the ocean, talks to moon and believes in magick. She loves animals and some people. Recently Lyssa has discovered that her niece, who lives in Texas, shares her love of writing. Despite the many miles between them, they video call often and talk about everything from puppies to Greek Mythology. She dreams of owning a castle with an enormous library where she can live, dream and write full time and invite her niece for long visits.

facebook.com/LinesByLyssa | instagram.com/LinesByLyssa

SHARIL MILLER

Sharil Miller is married with two beautiful daughters and three handsome grandsons. She loves photography as well as writing and tends to look at the world in a unique way, capturing moments and memories not only through the lens but through her pen as well. Sharil is adventurous and loves to travel. Three of her most favorite places for fun and adventures are Key West, The Outer Banks, and Myrtle Beach. She loves to go camping and has a cute retro camper to take time away to relax and refresh her soul.

T H SMART

T H Smart is a writer, poet, and visual storyteller. Both creative and strategic, she is as comfortable in the boardroom and training room, as she is in her home studio creating visual and written art. Her love for all things beautiful (shoes included) inspires her writing and artistic creation. By sharing the beautiful messages that skewer her heart, she hopes to stir up others in love so they too might be strengthened and inspired to run after the plans and purposes for their lives. She shares her suburban home in Cape Town, South Africa with her husband, daughter, and three furry friends. Learn more about her and her writing projects at www.warriorforworthiness.co.za and follow her Smart Musings on Facebook (https://www.facebook.com/SmartMuser/), Instagram (https://www.instagram.com/thsmart_smartmuser/) or LinkedIn (https://www.linkedin.com/in/thsmart/).

WHITNEY REID

Whitney Reid is a dreamer from a small southern town in Kentucky. She is a restless thinker and avid writer. Her passion for prose was ignited in college where she enjoyed literature and creative-writing classes. She shares an open heart and mind with a Facebook blog titled, "Arcane Angel" which contains soulful and enlightening musings. Her works often strike a chord of encouragement, and connection that welcome you to journey and dream with her.

MICHELE McKENNA

Michele McKenna began to write when she lost her Grandparents consecutively in 2016 and 2018. Dealing with severe depression, anxiety and trauma, she found writing as a way to escape and calm her through those episodes. Through her grief, she found a talent she didn't know she had. Writing grounds her. Her poetry and short stories are about loss, grief, brokeness, strength, weakness, vulnerability, getting in touch with your past and present self. While at the same time expressing raw unfiltered honest emotions & thoughts, searing passion, femininity, sensuality, romance, love, the darkness within, and also the endearing light. By expressing herself through her writing, it not only helps her, but she hopes it will help others feel connected to someone who understands, and help them feel not so alone in how they feel. One day she dreams of roaming the halls of a Gothic Victorian castle and finding a secret 2 story library walled with vintage and early editions books where she can sit in a leather chair and write. For now, you can find her at her Facebook Page 'Simple Elegance' facebook.com/Michele.SimpleElegance/.

SAVANNAH STOVER, THE SCARLET WIDOW

Savannah Stover, aka The Scarlet Widow, is a Nashville-area poet. Widowed from her high-school sweetheart, left to raise their 7 babies alone, and escaping an abusive relationship post-loss, she now writes of love, erotica, loss, and on becoming.

Social Media: Instagram @widowinred; Facebook: Savannah Leigh

SARAH HALL

Sarah Hall is an indie writer residing in Adelaide, Australia and has been writing poetry and prose for several years. Sarah is the owner and sole writer at Sarah's Collection of Scar's on Facebook with plans to release her own collection of work in the near future.

Sarah is a featured author in the "Rise From Within" and "As Darkness Falls" poetry anthologies by 300 South Media group and is a co editor and featured writer in "Rise Up Rabid Souls" poetry anthology by Ship Street Poetry.

Sarah writes powerful, emotive, raw and sometimes dark pieces. Her works are often inspired by her survival of domestic violence and other personal experiences in life, love and loss. You can find her at facebook.com/sarahscollectionofscars/

STEPHANIE MUELLER

Stephanie Mueller is an elementary multilingual teacher by day and a poet by choice. She finds inspiration in the human connections she makes with the families with whom she works and in mother nature's humble beauty. She currently enjoys small-town life in Wisconsin with her daughter and two feline fur babies. She has been blessed to have her words previously published online with Elephant Journal and in a recent anthology entitled, As Darkness Falls, orchestrated by 300 South Media Group. To read more, please visit her blog at https://samuellerblog.wordpress.com

VALERIE LEYDEN-MORFFI

Valerie (Whiskey + Empathy) is a full-time working, single mother (recently married), raising her son in downstate New York, in the foothills of the Catskill Mountains. She is a passionate soul, with a zest for life, who loves and feels things in a big way, highly attuned and sensitive to her surroundings. Valerie developed an affinity for the written word at an early age.

As an adolescent, writing became a catharsis. Restless, and a bit rebellious, Valerie finished high school early, graduating with her A.A. in Liberal Arts, at 18. In 2005, she earned her B.A. in Psychology, graduating Magna Cum Laude.

Other passions include cooking, photography, traveling the world, being a mother, singing in the car, Irish coffee, and enjoying a good whiskey and cigar night! Valerie is a lover of the creative arts… all her writings are raw and real, coming from life experience and the depths of her soul.

Publications and Additional Links to Valerie's Writing:

You can find more of Valerie's work on Facebook (facebook.com/whiskeyandempathy), Instagram (@whiskeyandempathy), and her Website (whiskeyandempathy.com), which is still a work in progress at this time. Valerie has also been published in the Rise from Within anthology by Jay Long (300 South Media Group) and Broken Hearts – Healing Words by A.B. Baird Publishing where one of her poems, "Light as a Feather," won the People's Choice award.

FIONA VAN ZYL

Writing is one of the great loves of Fiona's life. As with all love stories, the relationship has not been without its challenges, heartbreak, and loss. It is also where she found herself and where her truth dwells. She is a believer in the healing power of stories, their uncanny ability to reach out to us when we need them the most. When we choose to listen to their voices we can be guided home, to the core of who we really are.

She is a teacher, writer and therapist living in London with her beloved husband and pooch.

EMMA GLEDHILL

Emma Gledhill feels as though a love of words, stories, and books have been a part of her, all her life. Books have always been a sanctuary. She tends to lean towards a more melancholy subject matter. She began to write as an adult, after the end of a marriage that she felt she had to escape from rather than end. Writing, mostly indirectly, about the experience and the person she became since, became a cathartic exercise. Coupling that with finding the man that is the other half to her soul gave her a well of emotion and perspective she often draws upon.

Being a happily married mother of two small children doesn't always allow her the time to write as she wishes but she wouldn't change that. However, it is why it means so much to have been chosen to participate in this anthology. Follow her on Facebook at facebook.com/PentoPaperC2G

IMPASSIONED HEART

Theresa (Impassioned Heart) is a lover of love and her greatest passion is that of the written word. She has been translating her soul through words for the past 4 years, as part of her personal journey of healing, spirituality and rising above a broken past. She is purely a soul poet with hopes to inspire love, light, and healing in others. Her first language is Afrikaans, a native language of South Africa and her love for writing inspires her to write in both Afrikaans and English. One of Theresa's poems has been published in an anthology raising funds for Children with Cancer and she has also been featured in the web magazine "Bharat Vision", as well as a South African anthology honouring women. She is in the process of writing a book with parts of her treacherous journey and hoping to have it published in 2022. You can find more from Theresa at facebook.com/ImpassionedHeart and instagram.com/impassioned_heart

EMILY JAMES

Emily James is the pseudonym used by Lori Weyandt. Lori's soul roams from the mountains of Pennsylvania to the mountains of North Carolina. She is blessed to share her life with her fiancé Brian, her daughter Kirsten, son-in-law Gage and her littlest love, her granddaughter Elliott Rose. You can find more of her writing on

facebook.com/akaemilyjames and instagram.com/akaemilyjames. her book, Inside These Walls is available now via Amazon

JODIE BENDER S.B.

An Ohio native, Jodie Bender was born an imperfectionist.

She has always loved the fact that poetry does not always have to follow the rules.

It does not always have to have structure, it can be messy and chaotic, and still be beautiful. As a child, she fell in love with and started writing poetry.

She found emotional and spiritual strength in putting her words down on paper. She will write every day, for better or for worse,simply because she views the world as an endless poetic verse. You can find her online at facebook.com/AuthorJodieBender.S.B.068843163448

JAY LONG

Jay Long is a New York based author, poet, and natural storyteller. He is the founder of 300 South Media Group and his vision for indie authors is to give them each a fair and level playing field to their traditional published peers. His creative voice can be heard throughout social media and online writing communities. Through his writing and work with other writers, he continues to establish himself as one of today's prolific voices and advocate of modern day writers. To learn more about Jay visit jaylongwrites.com or you can follow him on Facebook at facebook.com/writerjaylong and @writerjaylong on Instagram Follow 300 South at facebook.com/300southpublishing and instagram.com/300southpublishing

JAMIE SANTOMASSO

Jamie Santomasso is a poet from Kansas City, Mo. A writer since the age of five, she has used the literary arts as a means to express her thoughts and feelings through the written word.

Jamie takes inspiration from both life experience and imagination to create vivid pictures of love, heartbreak, fantasy, darkness, and other residual works. Her works have received praise for their ability to evoke emotion, paint pictures, and tell stories that the reader can fully immerse and lose themselves in.

Jamie has been published in several online and print productions, including anthology works from Impspired, the Rio Grande International Poetry Festival, 300 South Media Group, and Open Skies. You can follow Jamie at facebook.com/SpiritOfTheSonneteer and instagram.com/SpiritOfTheSonneteer

MEL

Mary Eileen Loterbauer (MEL) writes to heal. As a paralegal by day. She often hears from people in crisis and she needs to be their beacon of light and help them find comfort in the darkest of times.. She writes for them and for herself. Her motto is " Life isn't easy, so let's help each other on the way through" You can find more of MEL at facebook.com/MelsSoulJourney/

JENNIFER TORVALSON

Jennifer Anne Torvalson is a former Rehabilitation Practitioner who has worked in many capacities from an inner-city counsellor to personal aide, to individual program plan writer, as part of government funding submissions. She has authored several pieces of prose, a musician's bio and, has written poetry since her youth.

Although the resident Canadian is hopelessly landlocked, much of her writing bespeaks of her love affair with the ocean and its ancient wiles.

Jennifer is a lover of simplicity and finding happiness in the smallest of things. She, however, is addicted to words and is a firm supporter of using 800 where 8 would normally suffice.

When not reading, writing, or enjoying music, she can often be found haunting used book stores or thrift shops and believes strongly in the beauty of imperfection.

Visit her via Facebook or at LostLass (Seaswept7) on Instagram.

AMY JOY

Amy Joy is a middle-aged maven addicted to alliterations, big words, and over-used clichés. She is also a certified yoga instructor, a mother of five, and a Nana of three. Her life's work is to help others see the best in themselves through her writing.

KERI KASAME

Keri Kasame is up and coming. They have lived in Austin, Texas since they were born and are deeply ingrained with the need to create poetry.

CHARLENE ANN BENOIT

Charlene Ann Benoit was born and raised in Newfoundland, Canada. She began writing poetry at the age of ten, and in 2004, she finished her first collection, entitled, Pieces of My Soul. In 2005, she completed her first novel, When Walls Come Crashing Down. Since that time, she has completed seven other books of poetry, In Memory Of (2005), Shattered (2008), Between the Lines (2019), In the Hearts of Gods, Monsters, and Men (2020), Blood, Tears and Coffee Rings (2020), Fairy Tales & Other Things I Tell Myself (2021) and The Road That Led Me Nowhere (2021). She has also written a children's book, The Littlest Prince (2015), which is awaiting illustrations, as well as a novella called Death's Daughter (2018).

Currently, she has several other projects in the works, including: The Skeptic, Whispers From Neverland, The Phoenix and The Dragon, In The Name of The Father, His Little Red Wagon, To Michael With Love, Love and Death on Jellybean Row, Redemption, and a trilogy entitled Blood Moon. You can find her at facebook.com/themidnightmoth and instagram.com/themidnightmoth

LEIGH ALISON

Leigh Alison has lived on three continents (so far) in her lifetime. She was born in Zimbabwe, grew up in South Africa, spent two years in the UK, and now lives in Massachusetts USA. Her Gypsy Soul loves exploring new places and traveling. She is one of those people that feels like she expresses herself best through the written word and she began writing in 2012. When she's not working as a Registered Nurse, or writing, she loves spending time with her two sons, the Love of her Life, and a menagerie of pets (she has four cats and a dog… for now).

To read more of her writing, you can find her at facebook.com/FlameLilyPoetry and instagram.com/flamelilypoetry

ERI RHODES

Eri Rhodes is a wife and mother of two boys in addition to being a writer. With one foot in reality and one foot in the fairy realm, this pixieish poet turns the pain of her past and the love in her present life into rallying cries for warriors and reminders to victims that they have the strength and courage to change their future. She writes with the same passion and whimsy by which she lives her life. In her spare time, she enjoys reading poetry and nonfiction, crafting, and studying true crime. She also enjoys sharing her love for writing with her youngest son and her love for true crime and the paranormal with her oldest. She is a fierce advocate for survivors of domestic and child abuse and for those living with mental illness.

You can find her online at facebook.com/pixiesecrets

MOLLY ASTRID EGAN (MAE)

MAE lives in Texas in the USA. She is the eldest of 3 and is a puppy wrangler and cat whisperer. Her cat Jackson likes to keep an eye on her to make sure that he gets his fair share of her attention. She loves school, swimming and playing the violin. When she has time, she likes to bake for her family. She writes poetry, short stories and is writing her first novel. Molly enjoys writing and long video calls to her aunt (also a writer) in Cape Town, South Africa. In the few hours that they are awake at the same time, they talk for ages about writing, mythology and how similar they are (despite a 33 year age gap). Molly is excited to realise her dream of being published for the second time in this anthology and feels that this is the beginning of a long and fulfilling writing journey. Follow her on Facebook at facebook.com/MollyAstridEgan

Thank you for reading Trails of Light. If you enjoyed it, please consider leaving a review. It truly helps the book and the authors be seen.
Also available from 300 South Media Group

Anthologies:

Rise From With – getbook.at/RiseFromWithin
Sunset Rain – getbook.at/SunsetRain
As Darkness Falls – getbook.at/AsDarknessFalls

Single Authors

Dawn P. Harrell
Seasons of a Sewer Girl – getbook.at/DPHSeasons

April Y Spellmeyer
Poetry Stained Lips – getbook.at/PoetryStainedLips

Emily James
Inside These Walls – getbook.at/EmilyJames

Ann Marie Eleazer
She's Magic & Midnight Lace – getbook.at/SMML

Margie Watts
Relfections of Me – getbook.at/ROM

Jay Long
Timeless Chatter – getbook.at/TimelessChatter
Eternal Echoes – getbook.at/EternalEchoes

ABOUT 300 SOUTH MEDIA GROUP

300 South Media Group's founder, Jay Long, saw a lack of one-on-one interaction for those seeking assistance when self-publishing their books. He noticed far too much misinformation being made readily available to would-be authors and companies trying to capitalize on the trust of inexperienced indie writers and self-publishers.

300 South Media Group began with the hope to level the playing field for indie writers and authors. For far too long self-published authors were considered hacks – and that is because many self-published books didn't take on a professional look or feel. Whether that was from lack of knowledge and understanding or not truly identifying the full scope of what goes into a successful self-published project. Jay wanted to offer helpful solutions for indie authors stepping into the public spotlight.

The heart and soul of the company is its dedication to providing indie authors with information and services to help ensure their projects are top quality and ready for their readers.

The vision 300 South stands behind is to guide and mentor determined writers towards the goal of being self-published, by assisting them to find the best course of action to achieve their goals. 300 South Media Group's services help ensure writers put out quality, professional products to the world.

Connect with Jay Long and 300 South Media Group on social media via Facebook and Instagram | 300SouthPublishing